I've Been
CONNED

BOOK FOR
DUMMIES

SUZANA THAYER

Tellwell Talent
www.tellwell.ca

ISBN
978-0-2288-7527-7 (Hardcover)
978-0-2288-7526-0 (Paperback)
978-0-2288-7528-4 (eBook)

Chapter One

SELF-REFLECTION

There is a time for love of family and life. I'm sure that you are aware of all the facets of daily life. When it comes to what you do, after a while it becomes normal, a routine that you just do every day. Being a mom for many years or a dad, for example, because no one is immune to things that just happen to us each day. We all wake up, do our morning rituals, eat, and get ready for the day. Not knowing at times what the day will bring, but there are always fires to put out or things that pop up unexpectedly, and we just take care of it to the best of our abilities and forge ahead to make the day go as smooth and as easy as possible.

I want to start off telling you a little about myself. I'm 63 years old, and I think analytically and intellectually for the most part. I have had many different jobs over the years, mostly because we moved a lot. I try to think outside the box, stay happy and cheery for my family and friends, and always help when I need to or am asked to. I believe I'm a true humanitarian by nature; I believe that everyone has good in them, and that some just might not know it yet and need a person to use as a sounding board. That's me the sounding board—ha ha, yeah; it can be a good thing but also a bad thing.

Many times people came to me for help even if I didn't know them; I would help them, my heart just went out to them. Mostly because I wear my heart on my sleeve. People are just naturally drawn to me and talk, as if I have known them their whole lives. Yes…that is because I care about people and somehow, they sense that from me as soon as they look at me.

Now I met my husband when I was 13, he was 12 and we just hit it off, from the first time we laid eyes on each other; so yes, I do believe in true love. I believed in love, we all do, or we hope for love to open the door one day into our lives so we can feel whole. Now I was married for 45 years to Jim, the love of my life. My dream man, my soulmate and my friend. It was him and I against the world. Both sides of the family resented the fact that we were together. Both of our mothers wanted us to pick sides…but which side to pick? We didn't pick either side, we made our own side together. It was the most logical move, really. Without thinking we became us, him and I against the world. We got married four days after his 18th birthday. We had both sides attend (he didn't want any of the parents there, I did, because that way they knew for sure, yes…we are married) in our small apartment in Scarborough on the 23rd floor, way up in the sky. I wanted both sides there just to prove to them we were legally married. Our oldest daughter was 10 months old at the time, and is in our wedding picture. I always believed being open and honest was the right way to treat others. You see, I hate lies and betrayal more than anything in life.

Now when we got married my husband worked in a factory, but always wanted to be a policeman. But he was still young and couldn't even apply for a job with them till he was 21, so he bided his time till he could apply. Just before his 21st birthday he applied and believe it or not he got a job with the local police department. We were so proud and it was an exciting time for him. Our home life was full of love, happiness, and joy. We were happy a couple, so much in love and being parents, we felt like we were on top of the world really. We did everything together. We enjoyed doing things as a family.

Now my husband ended up going to police college; it was paid by the police department and he was paid to go. He spent three months in Almer for the course and passed. When he got back, he was on the road taking care of people; that's why he wanted to be a policeman by the way, because he wanted to help people. I thought that was a commendable reason for him to be one and I backed him up 100 per cent. I think you would do the same as I did, for sure.

Everything was going great and there is a reason for this story, so bear with me please. He was working, and just after about 18 months of being hired on we had a very tragic incident. You see, my husband was on the police baseball team; he was up to bat and the pitcher threw a wild ball. I was tending to our second daughter at the time as she was just a few months old. I knew he was at bat, and I heard the sound of a pop, like he had hit a long drive ball out of the field. I turned to look and there was my husband lying on the ground, motionless. I darted over to him and he started to stir a bit, but I knew he wasn't right. Without thinking I ran off the field and darted to get the car. I even drove it right onto the baseball diamond so that we could load him in the car. Funny thing, none of the police officers even thought to come help me with him.

Off I went to the doctor's office a couple of miles away; I knew he had to be seen right away. When I got him there the doctor said he needs to go to the hospital, but instead of saying we are sending him by ambulance he gave me the option to drive him, and I said yes, of course I will take him. They had called ahead to Newmarket to expect us there. When we got there, they started to assess the injury; they decided to send him to a hospital in Toronto that specialized in head injuries.

He went by ambulance, and I drove to the hospital to be with him. The specialist came in, who happened to be the top neurosurgeon in Canada, and he told me that he had a star fracture to the skull and cerebral hemorrhaging, and that he would have to do burr hole surgery to relieve the pressure on his brain. But now because of the medications given to him, they had to wait till they had dissipated out of his system. Then due to negligence (an intern who felt bad that my husband was in pain), two hours before surgery an intern gave him a shot of pain killers, which delayed him being able to have the surgery. In the meantime, the surgeon gave him pills to counteract the swelling on his brain. Because of this, they canceled the surgery altogether, as for some reason the swelling was reducing on its own. But he would have to take these pills forever.

He ended up having paraphasia, which is something a two-year-old would have, where they have difficulty saying words. He would twist the words around; like instead of Pontiac he would say Pontipac. He had to go for speech therapy for six months. At least he had job security, which was lucky because he had only just passed the probation period. So they couldn't do anything but pay for his work and benefits. Now I'm coming to why I told you this; you see, that head injury changed the man I married.

He became abusive and angry all the time (but only with me). It didn't matter what it was for, he was just angry. If the children did something he didn't like he wanted to strike them, and I would jump in front of them and get the blows. I had to protect them, and also save my husband somehow. I didn't know what to do. I couldn't tell his work because he was a police officer, after all. Both sides of the family hated each other and would have loved for him and I to break up. I was embarrassed to tell our friends because they were friends to both of us, so you see I had no one to confide in at all. I was alone on this one, without help or aid. I also mostly believed in our vows: for better or worse, in sickness and in health. I had his back. So logically I had to help him, protect him, and above all love him, till death do us part. Also, after he was cleared to go back to work he was warned that a sudden blow to the head would kill him. So that was playing on my mind for the 25 years he was on the force, too. Because according to him, the pain was so bad that he started drinking. He became a closet alcoholic; yes, and a bad one at that. He was an angry and abusive drunk, and I lived with that for the whole time he was on the force.

I think you're starting to see the picture I am trying to draw for you. He was jealous of every man that showed me any attention, on top of everything else. I ended up only being allowed to go to work, home, and to buy groceries, nothing more. Oh, and to the liquor store. I was used to abuse and being mistreated; it was my new norm.

My husband passed away on December 21, 2016, and my life stopped that day. I was lost and alone. Basically, I hid from the world after that, till the spring of 2021.

It is important to look at who you really are. Knowing yourself is a key way to prevent a con from happening. A good exercise here would be to write down things in your past, good and bad, to help you understand who you are. Please take the time for yourself, because the people running a con are going to want to know everything about you. Yet they won't tell you anything intimate or personal about themselves.

Chapter Two

FIRST CONTACT

Now to tell you the why and the how of how I was conned. What happened to me? I'll tell you in hopes that you will learn from what I uncovered only after I realized it was too late to fix the damage the con did to me. Please take note of this because I don't want you to go through the pain and suffering I had to go through, and still am going through to this day. It was almost four and a half years after my husband passed away. As usual I was in my room, keeping away from my family, basically keeping to myself. I felt numb and was feeling very uninvolved with everything. Basically I felt like I was only existing, but I didn't realize that till much later, because I wasn't aware of my own thoughts.

It was the spring of 2021, an early summer day. I'm an early riser and went on my Facebook because that is how I see what my children are up to. That's when I noticed a request from the person I will call The Good Doctor. I was attracted to his looks, to be honest. I wanted to see what he was about; I found out he was a doctor. Wow, a doctor! A neurosurgeon, at that!! Yes, that intrigued me a lot. I love a man with a brain. In all honesty I had a sexual attraction to him almost instantly. That to me was something I never felt in my life towards another man except my late husband, and I really wanted to get to know him. He was a widower, just like I was a widow, so I felt an instant connection before I even accepted the friend request from him. It felt like we had things in common, really. I thought to myself that maybe we could be friends.

I even started thinking maybe I could find someone who would love me for me, be there for me, and I could love them too. This was something I really wanted more than anything. I wished for it a couple years after my late husband passed away. I had it written down on a paper; it was my wish list: to have someone again to make me feel whole. I'm sure you have felt that way, too. We are human, after all, and we all have needs. I was captivated from the get go; wow, a doctor and a humanitarian working for the UN on a diplomatic mission. When I read that he had been a widower for six years, and had lost his wife and daughter in a tragic car accident, I thought to myself, he knows how I feel. I should talk to him. I thought maybe he could help me in my situation, and I could help him the same way. So, I accepted his friend request. However, I really didn't think he would talk to me. I figured this was a mistake, he was not going to accept me as a friend, as I to him was just a simple plain ordinary woman.

Now, this was kind of a surprise to me. No sooner did I say yes to the friend request, than he texted me back almost instantly. It was like a heartbeat away. He said hello and said that I was beautiful and he had to know me. Well, I laughed and said that picture is really old lol I'm old. It was a picture my sister put on for me when she set up my Facebook, from when I was in my 20's. He said well how old are you? I said 63. He said well so am I 63. That's not old. I said that's not what I look like at all. He kept saying, you are beautiful. I don't care what you look like now, you are beautiful. Well, I don't know about you, but those words did seem nice to hear. Don't you think? When was the last time anyone said that to me? I was already liking him, being naïve. Well, in honesty it has been many years, too many years really. I liked the fact that this guy was kind of flirting with me. Wow, a doctor FLIRTING WITH ME. That was something I hadn't had in a very long time. So now what do I say to this doctor who seems to be coming on to me, in a way? I thought okay, well I will have a friend, someone who knows what I am going through.

I basically got my composure back in the situation, and proceeded to tell him, listen, for one thing I'm not looking for a relationship. I am not ready for one was going through my mind. This was so new to me. I never thought that I would ever want to start something just for me. I was busy watching my grandchildren, helping my family, doing what was needed to help people. How can I even think of myself when I am needed to help those around me? I said to him, look if you're a con trying to con me out of my money for me forget it. It's NOT going to happen. You can just stop NOW.

I asked him how did he find me? He said he was looking for a relative and came across my name. He said he felt he instantly had to know me. Remember, I felt that too; plausible, right?

Well, then he started saying, look, we were meant to meet, we belong together. God has made us meet. We are somehow connected. It's fate. I told him it was an accident, I shouldn't have clicked on his name and that I was very sorry. But he persisted; he didn't stop, just kept going on about what a beautiful person I was. That I have something special to offer. When a man does this, you somehow become powerless because in fact, you really didn't know how lonely you really were. In just a few quick sentences, he has you in a very good spot for him, one that is going to in time take your breath away. He now has your full and undivided attention. Now he keeps on going, he changes the subject and starts asking questions about you. Here are a few of the questions he asked me:

What's your favorite color?

What's your deal breaker?

Do you work?

Do you have children?

What do you do for fun?

Where do you live?

Do you own your own home?

Now I did answer him honestly, but I did ask the same questions back to him. Some he answered, and some he omitted. The one question that stood out was my biggest deal breaker. I told him I could not tolerate lies and betrayal. He jumped in and said that he was the same way, that he hated that above all. When I asked him about his wife, he said that it was too tragic, and he had to go for therapy for a long time because the trauma was so hard on him. He said he doesn't even want to think about it because it was too painful for him. Then he said something very strange, which I didn't believe at first; he said he was very rich and that he would never ask me for money. He did say that after his wife died, he signed a agreement with the United Nations for a nine-year contract, and that he has been there for six. But now that he met me, he wanted to retire and be with me forever.

I really did believe that he had signed a long contract. He seemed so genuine that he was very hurt after his loss, that it was something he didn't care about. You see, I felt the same way, I just was going through the motions of existing, really. The trauma is very real. So, I believed him.

My thought at this point was why would someone of his stature want someone like me. Well, he then ended up spending several hours texting me; he apparently owned several houses, and sent me pictures of the houses so that I could see them. He also sent a picture of himself sitting in a white coat at a desk, so I could see what he looked like. He wanted to make sure I knew he had money; for a long time, I didn't believe him and I thought he was just giving me a line.

After a while he said we are connected, we are meant to be together. It's fate, God wants us to be together. That was why he said we met. He said he knew I was the one for him, that he was told this, by God. He was very consistent with his words; then he asked me if I had Hangouts. Well, I didn't even know what it was, I'd never heard of it. He said he would send the information to me and how to download it. He said being who he was, he couldn't stay on Facebook because of the terrorists. So The Good Doctor insisted that we chat in Hangouts, which is used by the military because it is encrypted and safe.

Out of respect for the person I believed to be a real doctor, I felt it was my duty to comply with his wishes; after all, he did seem quite nice and caring to me. I had to get to know him, if you follow me. In a way I was becoming quite infatuated with the man. So, I complied and open an account with Hangouts and accepted him into my life, so to speak.

Chapter Three

HANGOUTS

He seemed very honored that I accepted his invitation for a one-on-one communication. Now he had me where he wanted me, in one sense—away from distractions like friends and family, to be exact. I just thought he wanted someone to talk to and still be safe in his part of the world, from terrorists.

Let's go through some of the information I have divulge so far, shall we?

1. First thing he did was pique my interest. How? Glad you asked; he sent a very attractive picture of a man that any woman would find handsome.

2. Then he kept saying how beautiful I was, even when I said I was old. I told him I was 63, but that didn't seem to bother him, because he was also 63, as he told me. I told him I was overweight still nothing. I said that I had false teeth and was damaged.

3. Well, he said it didn't matter what I looked like, that it was fate. He said that it was meant to be, and that we were

connected. He said the three words that make any woman feel a soft spot in their heart: I love you.

4. I told him I wasn't a normal-minded woman, that I look at life differently and that I care about people, that I look for the good in everyone. I said in a sense I was a humanitarian. He said that I was just like him.

5. I told him I didn't like liars and betrayal, he said he the same way.

6. He asked me to connect to a site that would keep him from harm and terrorists; I did just as he asked.

7. He said that he believed God has brought us to be together, and that it was truly love.

8. He used the love word a lot, and soulmate and that fate kept saying it was meant for us to be together.

9. He had to determine whether I had some money.

This all happened in a four-week period; I was starting to fall for him bigtime. But saying I love you back was something that did not come out till the fourth week. Once I said those words was when he started saying he wanted to retire and that he wanted to spend the rest of his life with me. He would send me morning messages that would melt anyone's heart;, at this point he had me not going on Facebook, and I wasn't watching TV. He had me on the phone texting him from when I was up right until I went to bed, and even in the middle of the night. I was very much in love with him at that point.

But how did he get me to fall in love online? How is it possible after a month of talking to someone to just fall in love.? Now, one thing about me, once I realized I was conned that bothered me and I needed to find the answers. I needed to know how he did this to me. Because to tell you the truth I felt like a fool. So, I started researching.

Then came the first request from him. He wanted me to write a letter asking for a leave for him. I thought okay, that's fine with me. He said he wanted to come to me and had applied for retirement. So, I did as he asked. About a week later I received a reply stating that I would have to pay just over $16,000 Canadian for the request to be processed. I argued with him about that and I even blocked him for two days. He sent me an email begging me to reconnect with him. Because my emotional state was anger and love it was easy for him to convince me to go back on Hangouts. I said to him I thought he was a con, and just using me to get money. He was there on my phone all the time so I couldn't even talk to my kids about it; he told me not to, and that he would be a surprise for them all. Little did I know that I was the one who would be surprised. He used the push me-pull me technique to get me to do his wishes; that made him very happy, and he would say heart-melting words to me. I had the money and I sent it to him through a wire transfer.

That was the start of how I was conned out of $206,000. So, if I were you, please keep in mind what they do to get you to where you can't stop, where you believe in the con more than you do your family. At one point I went to the bank to try and validate him, but they were no help at all.

Now how did he persuade me to do all this? Let's look at one of the first steps of a con. They need to get your undivided attention. How, you may ask? This is the answer to one of the most crucial parts of his plan. Well hold on to your seat, it's very ingenious. They use (whether it is a man or woman) a substance we all produce in our brains, that cons you to think you're in the most beautiful happy place of your life. It's called the *dopamine effect.*

Chapter Four

WHAT IS DOPAMINE?

What is dopamine, you ask? Well, this is what it is and how it works. I choose to give you detailed information right now; please read all the information, because I am going to give you facts to understand how it works. Because the remorse you're going to feel later if you don't listen to my words will be devastating. If you don't understand why things are happening to you, I don't want you to feel the detrimental effects in any way shape or form that happen when someone is trying to con you like I have been conned.

The major reason I am writing this book is to save someone else from the pain, torture, and humiliation of what happened to me. It has changed my life dramatically. Some would turn around and give up on themselves. Many have lost homes, family, friends, so that's why I am trying to tell you about this from the depths of my heart. I care about humanity and people. These people aren't doing this to make you a better person, it's just to fill their wallet with money. I am stressing this with all sincerity, care, and love, so please don't miss any of this.

Definition of Dopamine:

Dopamine is a neuromodulations molecule, often mistaken as a neurotransmitter, that plays seral important roles in in cells. It is an organic chemical 8, (that is naturally produced in our brain) of the catecholamine and phenethylamine families. Dopamine constitutes about 80% of the catecholamine content in the brain. Wikipedia

Formula: CaH11NO2
Iupac Id: -(2-aminoethylbenzene-1-2-diol

Preceptors D1-D-2D3-D4-D5 TAAR1

Precursor: Phenytgalanine, tpyrosine, and L-DOPA
Metabolism: MAO, COMT
Molar mass: 153,181 g-mol-1
Target tissues: System-wade
Side effects if /dirpameni include:
irregular heartbeats
nausea
vomiting
anxiety
headaches
chills
goosebumps
shortness of breath

Infusion

DOPAMINE is given by intravenous Ivy infusion. Low dose affects one to five MCG/ kg/minute Iv to increase urine output and kidney blood flow. intermediate dose affects 5 to 15 mcg/

kg/minute Iv to increase kidney blood flow, cardiac output, and contractility, add heart rate.

Excess

Having too much Dopamine-Or too much dopamine concentrated in some parts of the brain and not enough in other parts-has been shown to linked to being more competitive, aggressive, to even having poor impulse control. it can cause you to have a condition that include ADHD, binge eating addiction and even gambling.

Blood pressure

Dopamine is an important regulator systematic to help your blood pressure by multiple mechanisms. It effects your fluid and electrolytes balance to its actions on renal hemodynamics and epithelial ion and water transport and also regulations the hormones and human humoral agents. Jan. 22,2019.

People also ask what is dopamine and what is it responsible for?

Dopamine is a type of neurotransmitter. Your body makes it, and your nervous system uses it to send messages between nerve cells. That's why it's sometimes called a "chemical messenger". Dopamine plays a very big a role in how we feel pleasure.

How does dopamine make you feel?

Dopamine is responsible for allowing you to feel happy, pleasure, satisfaction, and motivation. Just like when you feel good that you have achieve something, it's because you have a surge of dopamine in running through the brain.

Does dopamine make you happy?

Dopamine often called the "happy hormone", dopamine results in you having a feeling of well-being. It's a primary driver of the brain's reward system, it spikes when we experience something such as pleasurable. May 3rd, 2021.

How does dopamine affect behavior?

Dopamine levels impact your mood regulations, your muscle movement, your sleep patterns, your ability to store and recall memories, your concentration, your appetite, and your ability to express self-control. When there is an imbalance in this chemical in your body, you as a person cannot function at an optimal level.

How do I get dopamine?

Here are the top ten ways to increase dopamine levels naturally.

1. Eat lots of protein, proteins are made up of smaller building blocks called amino acids.

2. Eat less saturated fats, fatty foods.

3. Eat probiotics. Such as yogurt.

4. Eat velvet beans.

5. Exercise often.

6. Get enough sleep.

7. Listen to music.

8. Meditate.

This is just an idea of certain things that increase the dopamine levels in your body.

What is dopamine made of?

A dopamine molecule consists of a catechol Structure (a benzene ring with two hydroxyl side groups) With 1 a mind group attached via an app ethyl chain. As such dopamine is the simplest possible catecholamine, a family that also includes the neurotransmitters norepinephrine and epinephrine. Foot note Health Direct there is a lot of information there, so check it out I used part of it to help with what you need to know

What are the love hormones?

High levels of dopamine and a other related hormone, norepinephrine, are released during attraction. These chemicals make us giddy, energetic, and euphoric, even leading to decreased appetite and insomnia-that means when we are so in love that you can't eat and can't sleep. February 14th, 2017.

Is high dopamine good?

You may not be aware of dopamine for its role in regulating motivation and reward-driven behavior. Larger amounts of dopamine will make you feel good. And this good feeling motivates you to repeat the behavior that triggers a good feeling. In this way dopamine is an important part of your survival. September 24th, 2019.

What are five happy hormones?

Serotonin, dopamine, oxytocin, and endomorphins are the happy hormones that promote positive feelings like pleasure, happiness, and even love. Hormones and neurotransmitters are responsible in all of essential processes. Like heart rate and digestion, but in your mood and feelings. May 21st 7th, 2020

What is a said hormone?

Production of serotonin-serotonin is a hormone that plays on your mood, appetite, and sleep; a lack of sunlight may lead to lower serotonin levels, which is linked and can cause you feelings of depression.

What are the four happy hormones?

4 happy hormones

1. Endorphins mainly helps one deal with stress and reduces feelings of pain.

2. Serotonin is mood stabilizer space well-being, happiness.

3. Dopamine is pleasure space motivational role in brain's reward system.

4. Oxytocin is a bonding space love and trust.

Can dopamine make you angry?

A new study shows that low dopamine levels can lead to aggressive behavior. Low dopamine levels in the brain may cause aggression, says a new study. Dopamine is linked to feelings of pleasure, gratification, and motivation June 11th, 2012

Does lying release dopamine?

If the results obtained suggest that when pathological liars lie, they released, the exact same amount of dopamine as honest people would; that there is no significant amount of dopamine released, and that the reward pathway is not involved, which means it's likely not that affected. September 8th, 2017.

Does exercise release dopamine?

It's possible that physical activity triggers a release of dopamine and serotonin, this can improve your mood. But there are other reasons why exercise plays a crucial role in the mental well-being. For example, exercise can be helpful for people who deal with anxiety and panic attacks. March 4th, 2020.

What is the dopamine diet?

1.   Daily foods such as milk, cheese, and yogurt.

2.   Unprocessed meats such as beef, chicken, and Turkey.

3.   Omega three rich fish such as salmon and mackerel.

4.   Eggs.

5.   Fresh fruits, vegetables in particular bananas.

6.   Nuts such as almonds and walnuts.

7.   Dark chocolate.

How can a woman produce dopamine?

I'm going to give you 8 ways to increase dopamine levels naturally.

1.   Eat lots of protein, proteins are made add of smaller building blocks called amino acids.

2. Eat less saturated fat.

3. Consumer probiotics.

4. Eat velvet beans.

5. Exercise often.

6. Getting enough sleep.

7. Listen to music.

8. Meditate.

Just a reference here so you know a lot of things will be duplicated in this. I apologize for the lengthy information session I am giving you here but it's crucial that you understand what the dopamine levels in your body do and how they are triggered. I will get to that if you just bear with me. But I don't really need to tell you much more about how dopamine affects your body or what can happen if something is triggered in you. The main reason I am expressing so much detail on this chemical in your body is because he (or she, obviously it could be a man or a woman) is using you.

Many people have been conned; watch out for them saying things like, have you eaten yet? I want you to stay healthy. You feel like they are really caring about you, but to understand this you must understand that this hormone is making you feel good. Yes, it is a wonderful feeling, yes you don't want it to end, yes, I know I am making it sound great too. But in honesty they will bleed you dry and then make you get money you don't have. At the moment of this feeling of happiness and joy, peace, tranquility, whatever you want to call it, this is the main reason of the beginning of your con. This is how he gets to you. This is how she or he constructs the concept of winning you over and creating a premise to make you believe you are truly happy when always in his presence. There's more involved to this and I will get to that. I do want you to realize that this is the beginning and the constant factor and the main reason that the con is using to infiltrate your mind, to cause you to do things you would never do in any situation whatsoever.

The only reason I'm doing this much detail though is so that you can really understand the purpose and cause of how someone did this.

Now I guess you're wondering how someone can manipulate your dopamine levels. How can someone just with words cause you to do things you would normally not do? How do you try and make any headway or understanding in the process used by such an individual? Well, I think I'm going to tell you enough so that you get an understanding of why I am being so methodical and chronological with what I am telling you.

The first thing I want to talk about is the actual con. The person that is conning you can even be a man, or a woman disguised as a man or a woman. What makes them try and get in your head, your thoughts, and your actions, so they can actually cause you to send money to that sad individual?

Well let's look at the individual for a minute. For starters they are or have a narcissistic personality. What is a narcissist? Who are they? What makes them tick? Yes, once again I am going to give you a little bit more information to make you a wiser individual, hopefully to help you and make you see how they work.

Chapter Five

WHAT IS A NARCISSIST?

According to the dictionary a narcissist is someone having an excessive interest in oneself and one's physical appearance.

What are the traits of a narcissist? (Ku. & Yu, 2010) Narcissistic personality disorders involve a pattern of self-centered arrogant thinking and behavior. They have a lack of empathy and consideration for other people. They have an excessive need for admiration. A lot of times people would describe a narcissist or someone who has narcissistic tendencies to have a cocky, manipulative, selfish, patronizing, and demanding personality. A narcissist also is someone that has a high IQ and is a very intelligent thinker. They consider themselves to be someone of great value, put themselves on a pedestal, make you feel like they are someone you should admire, respect, and devote all your time and effort to.

The reason I'm saying this is because you don't know if it's a man or a woman that is speaking with you. They put on a fake persona. They have done a lot of studying about the individual, the career, the atmosphere. They studied the individual's life so that they can take on that person's identity. They want you to believe with all your heart and soul that you are talking to that individual, the one whom you deem to be that person. Their behavioral patterns start to mimic the individual that they are portraying. To understand this individual would be totally insane for you to try and do. And there are many reasons why I'm saying this to you, I will explain that in a second. But you are talking to someone who can manipulate your mind using words and phrases that cause your dopamine levels to increase and change your cognitive abilities. They change how you believe your values are and who you are because they make you believe that you're their world. They literally get you high on yourself and involve your emotions, both good and bad. Yes, I will explain that in more detail because that is one of the other keys they use to enhance your dopamine levels, to the extent that you would do anything for them, even die for them.

To me this is a very sad statement of honesty. For what they have done to me or what this gentleman did, who I believed was a doctor in the military on a humanitarian mission to save people's lives, who would aid and assist others by risking his own life for these people. And eventually he asked me to save him, but we'll get to that, I promise. I just want you to be aware of what you are dealing with and who you're dealing with. It may not be as simple as you'd think; they don't really love you. That is the saddest part of this whole tale. Because one must understand you as an individual and they do try and get in your mind big time. They want so much information from you and at one point when they wear you down, they will get that information. They will get into your head, use thoughts, feelings, and your emotions to the extreme, so I want you to be aware of that. I want you to have the idea of what this person is like and what they're willing to do just to get money from you.

Chapter Six

INNER SELF

This part is very hard for me to talk about really, because of what this individual did to me. For starters, I want you to know a little more about me at this point: who I am, what makes me tick? Because this narcissist said that God is his savior, to have faith and believe. So, in my head, because this narcissist was getting in my head, he made me believe without a shadow of a doubt, that I really loved him, and believed in him, and cared for him. I'm not proud of that by any means. I am a true believer in God, my heart and soul are his forever, and as a matter of fact, I believe God is the one giving me the strength to write this book.

There was only one man in my life since I was 13 years old; we met before high school. I know I was young, and I didn't know what love really was back then quite honestly. I didn't know what a man could be like, what a man could make you feel like, how good it was to have someone who put you up on a pedestal and made you feel like a queen. I didn't know that type of man even existed. I didn't think it was possible. I only had one man in my life, and he ended up with a star fracture to the skull with a cerebral hemorrhage four years after we were married. That changed who he was; he had a lot of anger and frustration because he couldn't talk right and that made him feel very inadequate. My husband became an alcoholic, a closet drunk, whenever he was off. And it sometimes trickled into days he had to work. I literally had to drive him to work, because of what he drank. But I believed in the sanctity of marriage to the point where I had to help him. The narcissist did find out about this information because I told him eventually and that also helped him play on my feelings.

There's a part of dopamine that I need to explain to you right now. The way to really play on your feelings is by changing your dopamine levels. How do you do that? How can you increase a chemical in your body using words to change your emotions? Words are the strongest force that anyone can use, and anyone can change your feelings by changing your dopamine levels. How do they do that? They end up first getting you by attraction to them physically with their looks, work status, the feelings that they expressed to you. They use beautiful and touching words about how they feel about you, plus, how they feel deeply about you in themselves. You will notice it, and you want to watch for that part. You must watch what they are doing; are they doing anything to make you feel better?

This great doctor did it, someone who I thought was a doctor and a surgeon to boot, which is kind of ironic since he was a narcissist and a fraud. But you must look at all the aspects of what's going on. You must take everything into account, and they're going to have you so overwhelmed that they're going to blindside you so bad that you don't know what hit you. And that's what I'm trying to do here; I am trying to show you what this individual will do to cause you to change who you are, and how they do it. The only way I can do this is by relaying my story to you, so that you have some understanding, some guideline, some recourse at some point to turn around and say, hey, I am being conned.

Everything that exist within your bones, in your heart, in your mind, and in your soul, this individual is going to try and change all that on you. Your abilities—he's going to utilize it to the extreme, he's going to try and make you look at everything through his eyes, to the point that you will focus on every aspect of how you're going to obtain money for them. My con artist kept saying, don't worry, once you've saved me, you're going to get every cent back, plus interest.

But there's something you don't know about me. I'm not about money, I have never been about money. Mine was always the well-being of others because I cared for other people. But in the process I realized that I really wanted someone to love me for me. I have helped a lot of people, given a home to some who were homeless without any remuneration whatsoever. I've given money to ones who couldn't pay their hydro, couldn't pay their rent, couldn't buy food. I wanted to see my children get ahead in life, so what did I do? I sold my house to my oldest daughter for about a third less than what the market value was, which was in the 6-digit figures. With the remainder of the money, I paid off vehicles for one daughter, bought windows and doors for my other one, paid for a central air system, gave money for schooling for one daughter because she wanted to change her career. I gave them most of my money, because I wanted them to have a good solid foundation while I was still here and alive. And I will tell you how that worked out in the end, once they found out that I was conned.

Therefore, I want you to know who the individual on the other end of the line is. I want you to have understanding so that you can feel mentally, I mean not emotionally, but mentally the ramifications involved in his process or her process, and how they try to guide your mind to an extreme really, because they do take you right to the edge until you say, hang on, what's going on, what have I done, what have I become, is it really me who is doing all these things? Because at some point you do end up losing yourself in the process. That is something I feel ashamed of, I didn't like that person I was looking at when I looked in the mirror. Before I was conned, I liked who I saw, I may not have liked my looks, which I'm pleased to say I had started changing prior to this so-called gentleman caller.

I just needed to express some of my feelings to you right now as I am writing this because my heart is in tears and a big part of that is even though I know he conned me, even now I knew he made me do things I would never have done, a part of me still loves that man—or woman, who knows, I really don't know! To be completely honest, my heart is still in love with him. Plus, I wanted it to be true. I wanted him to come to me more than I wanted anything in life. I fell deeply in love with this so-called Good Doctor and it still hurts. But the truth is he was not the person he let on to be, He was not the man who wanted me for me, his end game all boiled down to one thing: MONEY. The biggest kicker of that is wanting to prevent this from happening to you.

In saying this, yes, it does sound like a fairy tale, something a woman or even a man would fall for. At the time you feel like you're in a world of fantasy, something you only dream of. It is beautiful, and if you want to lose every cent plus go into debt, then by all means stop reading this. But in fact you are being played. You are being used. No more or less. The person on the other end of your conversation is only taking you to the cleaners.

Now I'm going to tell you more about what he did and how he did it, in further detail. You will learn what happened to me so please keep reading on, please try and understand what I went through because if I can save you, then I've done my job.

Chapter Seven

FOLLOW THE BREADCRUMBS

This is where things get interesting. Now, so that you understand a little more about who I am and how I was manipulated, this is the next part of my tale.

So now we've established that I am in Hangouts, chatting with this guy who seems to be admiring and adoring me from afar. What was he going to do? Next, how was he going to do it, what was he going to say? So where do I begin? Might as well begin at the top, right? Well here, so let's get curled up on the couch, let's put our phones to the side, turn them off if you must, because if you're in the process of being conned, trust me; I don't think you're going to want to miss this part.

So here I am in Hangouts, talking with a doctor who's a humanitarian for the United Nations, working on a diplomatic mission. He had already told me that he had signed a contract for nine years and he's already done six of those years. He had three years left of his term. Now just a little detail about him, because I didn't really get a lot of detail out of him in all the conversations we wrote over the months of communications, he was very secretive about himself. That was a warning sign, that he never gave details. He did tell me near the beginning that his wife and young daughter were killed in a very tragic car accident, for which my heart went out to him. He said that it changed his life tremendously, and was a tragic event that caused him to withdraw from life for several months. These were all lies.

The other thing I found out about him, was that he told me was that he had a son in the military, and that they communicated through Gmail. However, during that time I was in communication with this man he had not heard anything from his son which was unusual, and he was worried about him. Now that made me ask him several times over, how's your son, have you heard from him? Because I was starting to have some concern for his son's safety. At first, he told me that sometimes his son, because of where he was, could not stop and possibly communicate with him. So, at first, he seemed fine with the fact that his son hadn't yet sent any news to him about his own status and safety. I did mention to him that no news is good news, especially when someone is in the military fighting a war, because they're quick in letting you know if something happened that was bad. He agreed with me.

So now you can see that first he did get some of my emotions going by involving his son, who he felt worried about. Sometimes in his communications he even displayed anger, saying that his son should be in touch with him. He continually showed numerous instances of his concern for his sons' safety. So, what else could The Good Doctor say to me about his life? He kept telling me that he was very wealthy, very rich, and was willing to take me anywhere I wanted to go. He did mention that he was looking for a woman who didn't have any baggage. Who had put their past behind them, now he had mentioned this several times over about baggage? He said he was too old to deal with baggage anymore. He said he was looking for a woman to share the rest of his life with, to love, honor, and obey. Someone that he could call his soulmate, the love of his life, and spend each moment till eternity with.

So, what does this do, because suddenly, he started talking to me like he was truly in love with me. Head over heels, that I was his true soulmate, that God put us together, that we were going to be a team, that we were going to be united, that we would touch each other, feel each other, hold each other, love each other forever. And then there is me, (going through my head) having only one man that I've ever made out with, who I ever knew or loved. I've been through some good times, bad times, and even worse times in my life with him. When suddenly, I have this man who's showing me affection, plus he's a doctor, a neurologist, that's showing me some compassion, some caring, some loving, understanding, not questioning what I do or how I do it.

Now in our conversations we talked about many things. I told him that I was taking pills, to help me sleep every night and even with the sleeping pills I wasn't sleeping right. But it was making me talk funny and I was saying things I don't even remember saying. Now he thought that was kind of odd, and worried for me (or more like worried I may say something that would stop his plan) at this point. So, what did he do? He convinced me into stop taking the sleeping pills. This was hard for me to do, in more ways than one because I ended up going cold turkey. He was cheering me on the whole time, saying you can do this, you've got the strength and courage to do it. Well, the first night I didn't take any sleeping pills, (I was taking the max amount you could possibly take) so the first night I only got 37 minutes sleep. Not a lot, but I made it through that first night, and was proud of myself. Didn't sleep anytime during the next day and he was telling me how proud he was me. of me. I didn't want to disappoint him. So, the next night I didn't take my sleeping pills again; well, I ended up getting an hour and 25 minutes, I think, of sleep. I know I was tired, yet he was telling me how proud he was of me and how much he loved me for having the courage and the stamina to just not take those pills.

As it was each day, I got stronger; each day I went without taking the pills, and each day I got a little more sleep, till one night when I was just completely exhausted, I ended up sleeping the whole night. That was a breakthrough and oddly enough after I did get off the pills, I was sleeping better—not taking them I was sleeping better. I had so much gratitude and respect for him standing behind me and cheering me on, saying I can do this, I can get myself away from those pills. And he kept using different terms to help, not the terminologies that only a doctor uses. He was very precise with his medical terms to an extremely convincing degree. And that's what made me think he was really a doctor; he would tell me I should eat because I wasn't eating much. He would suggest which foods I should eat; I was eating a hardboiled egg for breakfast and a cup of tea with no sugar. He'd be upset if only I had a tea because he said that's just hot water, (he seemed to show true concern for my health and safety). And he said to me, well, once he got here, he was going to get me off all those pills. I'm going to make you feel good about yourself and you're not going to need anything, just me, he said. He said he would save me and make me the best person I could be, basically. I started to adore him, I started to fall for him big time, I knew it wasn't an infatuation anymore. I was truly in love with him at this point.

Then one day he said he really wanted me, I mean wanted me, the way he was talking and asked me if I wanted to have sex with him. Wow, I hadn't had sex in maybe 15 years and being a woman who was right into sex for many years with her late husband, and a man I had come to respect asked me that. The only man I ever had sex with was my husband, and I was having very deep feelings for this gentleman. He was sexually arousing me with his words; his words had very strong connotations behind them. (I am a lover of unique and odd words) you really must look at what the words mean and are saying to expand and grow your mind and your soul. So, we started sexting, he would have some porn videos but before we get into that I just want you to see something that he wrote me, and this is the way he wrote me all the time, gave me sweet little thoughts of how he was feeling about me, that made me believe that he was truly in love with me as I was with him. This is one of the things he wrote me, and it is word for word. This is just an example of how he would talk to me every morning because he always sent me sweet messages to start each day and here's how it went:

Honey let's start the day with the world's biggest truth my love for you. I love you. My joy. You are my sunshine and that is why texting you in the morning is a very first thing I do. I will not refrain from telling you today how ardently I adore you. Your presence has made this Earth an Eden for me. wherever you are, you are ever you are. Even during the darkest nights, you hold me with all your love, and you assure me with so much hope and peace. The flowers dance with the gentle morning wind, as my heart dances with my love for you. Good morning my queen! God has given us another day filled with more blessings than we can count. Every night I go to bed wishing for sweet dreams for you. But when I wake up, I am glad that our love is a reality. I am blessed to be able to spend each day with you. I love you, and I can't wait until we meet each other. If it's never an ordinary day when I start it with you. Thank you for blessing me daily, my Angel. Rise and shine my love. The sun is up, and the birds are singing to let you know just how great this morning is. Good morning my joy, I hope my words brighten your day. I love and care about you so much, my Princess with a heart and a kiss.

So, you tell me, with something like that, wouldn't it would touch your heart, and make you feel that someone really cared about you? To me I was very touched by it, very consoled, and confronted with joy and love. You see, words are a beautiful thing, (they can also be used to hurt you or abuse you), especially if the motives worked for the right reasons. So yes, did I sext with him. I did, but now I don't feel proud of it, but at the time I felt like I was on top of the world. Going back to what I was telling you before, dopamine was the route that made me feel that way. You see, meds can reduce your happiness hormone and certain foods can increase it. So, note how he was transitioning my mind in the path of his desires.

This is going to feel like you're on a big ride, one that just seems so phenomenal, and you feel so alive. That's when I realized how much I am missing in my life. I needed someone to love me for me and I thought I had found that person, so yes, I did sext with him, I did. And I enjoyed it, we both came and how we did it was amazing, I don't know if you really want to know, but I'll tell you for me to it was amazing and I felt like I was on the biggest ride of my life. I really believed that I had found my true love.

For the first time in my life, something I really didn't have with my late husband, I should say. I felt that was life too short, I could see around me everyone being happy with someone. I was looking at people differently; older couples walking in the park, walking by the waterfront, happy. That was some place I used to go all the time when I was talking with him on Hangouts. I would describe what it was like there, I would tell him how the water was, what the trees look like, how the grass grew, what it smelt like, the breeze, the sun hitting my body. There were so many things that I felt so alive with because I had someone who actually seemed to care about me more than my late husband, did because he worked, was injured, abused me, was a drunk for 20 years of his life (obviously I was there to be had, I admit it okay) but the thing is, I was seeing life in a completely different way with this guy. I felt like I was on top of the world for the first time in my life. Dopamine has that effect on people. It can make you feel so high in a way that no drug on this planet can do for you. He said because he was a doctor, he was going to take care of me, get me off all my medications, get me off my painkillers because he thought I was taken too many of them. He genuinely showed a lot of care and concern for how I felt, what I needed and what I wanted. It was like he listened to every word I was saying, every move I was making, everything I was doing. He said I was the woman for him.

I need to back up for a minute to let you know something that I did daily, that he just seemed to admire a lot. When I first started talking to him, I told him I love to walk and that I love the waterfront. So, daily, I would always go down with my car to the lake. I would go on to the peninsula, where I would walk along the waterfront, and they have these trees there, weeping willow trees, that I just adored and loved them, because it reminded me of my father because he loved weeping willows. So, as I walked along towards where I go to the end of the peninsula, I would always raise my hand and high five the weeping willows as if I was saying hello to my father. I would describe these moves to him, he just seemed to be on every word I was saying, as if he really was in a war zone where all he was seeing was death and destruction. I would tell him what the wind was doing, what the sun was doing, how it felt, I could feel it just penetrating my body. I would describe everything to him.

I was there so often at the waterfront that there was a batch of ducks that would always follow me, I would never feed them however, but they seem to be entranced by me and enchanted in a way, I guess. I would always say hello to everyone that walked past, and men were starting to notice me for the first time in my life. And I would tell him that too, and he would genuinely seem to be jealous of these men. I would get to my usual spot where I would sit; I just close my eyes and listen to the water as it rushed along hitting the rocks along the beach. How to wind would gently whisks past my body. I would get so descriptive, so that he could visually see it. But he got angry once with me when I ended up sending him a picture on Hangouts and said that I could have him compromised and hurt or killed by the terrorists, because of that one move, because pictures were not allowed.

So yes, I was very entranced by him, and it showed on me as well because more men started noticing me and he kept saying well they better leave you alone because you're my woman. He would always sound so jealous when I had mentioned it to him, but I was an honest person and wanted to tell him exactly what was going on. But when I went to the waterfront one of the things I always did was I had my radio blaring, looking cool and I loved it. Some men would see me drive up in my car with my radio going and like the song that was playing or something, they would come up and talk to me before they even got out of the car. I was changing and I like those changes that I was making for myself. I have lost over 50 pounds; I used to dress frumpy, which my son ended up pointing out to me. And that also was where things started to change. Because I did tell my son that I was talking with someone on the Internet. And he did not like the fact that I was talking with anyone about him. So, you see there are many things that are slowly starting to show here for you of how someone can take advantage of you without you even realizing that what's happening.

Chapter Eight

LET THE MONEY GAME BEGIN

PART ONE

So, things started slowly changing once we started sexting, in the second month of meeting, suddenly, he asked me for a favor. He said that he wanted to get out of the military early and retire, because he was 63 and he was tired of having to do what he was doing. He was scared for his safety, his health and well-being. He was afraid he was going to die. What ended up prompting this was one day he said they had a terrorist attack at the hospital. He then proceeded to say that he ended up hiding in the corner of the room because the terrorists came in. They were trying to kill people especially doctors, and he was fearing for his life.

In one way he was being melodramatic I guess and really trying to show that things were bad there and getting worse by the minute. He did sound like he was generally scared for his own safety and well-being. So, at this point what do you? Think what you would do and I kind of was scared for him at that point. I really wanted to help him in some way if I could. I didn't say what can I do to help you or anything like that, but I was scared that he was going to die. That somehow one of these days the terrorists were going to get him. So, after that happened, he asked me a question, he said would I mind writing a letter for him, because he could only go on leave if someone writes a letter for him. He said that his late wife used to do it. He got a little sullen with his words at the time, as if he was having a flashback of memories from his late wife, just in his words it came out, I can't tell you exactly what they were because I don't have all the words now. But you know what I'm talking about when I say that. There are many things that do happen and the way he was describing what was going on sounded horrifying.

And I kind of said to him at that point are you okay? Just that I wanted to help him. At this point I was fully and deeply love with him. It was just a letter, what harm would that do? I was in the strong belief that he was my true love. I wanted to be with him for the rest of my life and spend every moment I can with him and be happy. I'm too old for all this anymore I can't do it anymore, he said. So, he asked me if I would write a letter for him to the United Nations asking for a leave to go and see his girlfriend. I said, well, I wouldn't even know what to write for you. He said to me that he would compose the letter for me, then send it to me to send to them. I agreed to that because I felt, well I don't want anything to happen to him because now I'm starting to really care for this man big time. So that afternoon sometime down the road he ends up writing a letter and sending it to me via email. I opened the email that he sent me, and I read the letters through. It was very well written very professionally done. However, he wrote on it not to go see his girlfriend, but he referred to me as his fiancée. I was stunned at this point, without even being asked. But I kind of let it slide, a little bit, and said okay I'm still going to send the letter off to them. If it saves him, then I feel I've saved a life. Then I indicated to him that I had sent off the letter on his behalf. He was very appreciative of the fact that I did it and I that I didn't even question what he had written on the letter. You know, it's like they can say one thing but that's not what they mean, or did he really need just someone to do it for him?

A couple of weeks went past; eventually I ended up with a letter back from the United Nations, saying that The Good Doctor was a very well-respected individual with the United Nations and with the amount of time and service that he had done for the country that his request for vacation was granted. However, there was a charge for this vacation process according to the United Nations, on their letter, that would have to be paid on his behalf to have him be approved for his vacation. This ended up being a sum of over $13,000 to have him be approved for his vacation leave, and I would have to pay that fee to have him get to me, apparently. Well, I was kind of stunned when I read the letter. I wanted to discuss it with him in further detail. When I did bring up the fact was when I brought up the point that he put down that I was his fiancée in the letter, it said that I had to pay $13,000 Canadian approximately for him to get this grant of leave.

In his defense, which was the first con, he responded without hesitation that he didn't know how the process worked, but I do know the only one that can let me leave or help me leave would be my wife. He said he put me down as his fiancée so that there wouldn't be any question from them, to let him leave and come to me. I didn't know that there was a cost attached to that, he said. And I said to him you said you'd never ask me for money, and that I said that was a deal breaker. And then we had a fight. Now at this point, here the dopamine level was a lot higher because all the beautiful words, compliments, expressions, desires that he was expressing to me in many ways and forms was at a high. But also, I did not want to pay any money for his vacation, and what enhanced the fact that we had a very huge argument was that he blocked me. That's when I started calling him a con and a liar, I said that he was deceitful trying to just take my money. Yeah, I think I would have learned at that point, that I was right, but my feelings for him were very strong. So, he had blocked me and now I was feeling a whole bunch of emotions.

NOTE: Another dopamine enhancer is stopping all communications. Don't talk to them at all, get them to think of you and only you are part of the con.

Was I doing the right thing? Was he real? Oh my God, did I do the wrong thing? But he was still on my Facebook, he hadn't deleted me off his profile yet. So, I sent him a text saying can we talk about this? Why would you block me like that? Wouldn't you know it, no sooner than I hit send he ended up sending me a text on Facebook saying, what's up sweetheart. As if nothing was wrong. Oh no, he used to call me babe not sweetheart, I apologize, I was always his babe unless he was upset with me. He'd call me by my real name Sue, in an abrasive use of my name, I guess, but in turn I was shooting him. He reinstated the chat on Hangouts so that I would go back and talk.

The funny thing about dopamine and your body, if you end up having an argument with someone you really care about emotionally, it increases your dopamine levels to an extreme high. And that gets you more in that happy mood that just makes you feel like you're so high, and if you think you're in love it's unbelievable. And one thing led to another, and he convinced me, because I did have the money in the bank to pay it for him. I thought to myself, well $13,000 isn't that much to help a man who I really care about at this point and I'm falling deeply in love with him. So, I assumed that by sending this $13,000 that he was coming to me regardless. I agreed to send $13,000, he also felt very happy and said to me let's do some sexting. So once again we did some more sexting, it seemed to make him happy after all. One of the things I did notice about his sexting, at first it was all words that were already written down, about what the acts were supposed to turn you on.

After a while it started changing where he started putting my name Sue occasionally in there, which kind of turned me on even more. I wasn't a babe anymore; I was being called something close to who I really was. And that also adds to your dopamine in your system. You can see how I'm telling you that the dopamine levels in your system can really change how you act and how you feel about a certain individual. But it's also how they talk to you and what they do to you that makes it work so well.

Even though the police checked and the information that they received proved he was a fraud, your mind at first has a hard time believing it. You wish it still to be true. But it never was, okay, you must trust me on that. Even though it is real to some degree in your heart because of your feelings, it is not real. Somehow, if this has happened to you, that is the fact that you must accept. To this day sometimes I still wonder if he really was true, and I know without a doubt that he was a con but I still struggle with it because it is painful.

Back to before I knew he was a con. At some point he decided that we're going to have sexting daily because apparently now I was sort of his fiancée. He hadn't asked me at that point until one day just before I received the UN's letter saying that they received the payment, because I ended up sending it via wire transfer. But a couple of days before I received a letter from the United Nations is when The Good Doctor decided to talk about getting married. Now I thought I was in love with him, of course I would love that, but I wasn't sure yet. He was setting the stage for the money con.

The UN sent information that The Good Doctor was approved for leave. However, the only way he can leave is to be married.

Now, they had already taken money from me. Remember, I was in love with him. So they had received the money and blah blah blah blah blah all the details and the protocols and all that stuff that apparently you must go through with the United Nations to achieve any type of response. One day we're sitting there talking about things that I did on my walk down to the waterfront and I started sending him pictures of the waterfront and what was happening, what it was like so that he could see something that was beautiful and pure and peaceful because I wanted to reassure him that there was more to life than the war zone that he was seeing there for the last six years.

So, as we were talking all the sudden, he said, I must ask you something. And I said okay what do you want to talk about, or what do you want to ask me. There was a pause, then all sudden I saw the little balls going up and down on my screen, that he was typing something and to my surprise what came out was, I am in love with you. I know that you're my soulmate and my true love. And then another text came up and it said these words will you marry me? Well, that took me by surprise like you wouldn't believe it just about knocked me off my feet, really, if you want to tell the truth I was kind of stunned and surprised when he asked me that. Especially since the fact that I had already told him that I have one of the worst bedside manners for any doctor. that you can possibly imagine when I was sick or in hospital for any type of surgery or whatever the case may be. But I was the best advocate for anyone who was in the hospital and doctors usually avoided me because of how well I would fight for the individual that was sick. Because that's what happened with my husband just before he passed away, he ended up in hospital with a very bad illness and needed surgery promptly. They were delaying treatment for my husband whose blood pressure was through the roof, sugars were through the roof, blood pressures were below normal that they had to tilt him upside down just to get the blood flow to the brain. and he had a cyst on his back which was causing all this to happen to him. I had to fight tooth and nail to get them to do something, which they ended up sending him for emergency surgery in Toronto. But they wouldn't tell me about it. I was trying to fight to get to Toronto so that I could be there when he comes out of surgery.

I had explained all that to him, he knew very well my feelings on doctors. However now I'm stuck with this one question. What do I say to this guy who's a doctor? He just asked me to marry him, it was like wow I almost felt like a princess. I felt honored and alive in a big way. And I sat there kind of scared, shaking, nervous, trying to figure out what do. I paused for a few more minutes thinking. He waited; he didn't say a word until I responded to that question. Then suddenly, my fingers started typing and I said yes, I will marry you. I thought how I could get so lucky to have a great looking doctor, a doctor I thought to myself, wow. I was nervous, scared, but wow a doctor wanted to marry me. I couldn't believe it, I had to read it three times I was shacking, this was real I said yes, yes, I will marry you. I felt so happy so alive that I couldn't believe it. I said to him well now that we really are engaged, can I tell my family about you? He took no time to reply and said no, let me be a surprise for everyone there, let's just surprise them ok. Plus, because I am a diplomate my safety is important, and you are the only one I am aloud to communicate, with so, please don't tell anyone. And because what he was saying made so much sense to me at the time I did as he asked. But everyone was noticing a change in me.

I was happy, upbeat, looking better, losing the weight I wanted to, was spending more time at the waterfront, everything. I was also on my cell phone practically all the time. At that time that seemed to bother my daughter-in-law and my son the most. because at this point, I was spending more time talking with The Good Doctor then I was spending with my grandchildren. But what is one to do, how is one to look at that and see what's happening. How did I know what was happening to me really, All I knew was that this good doctor, who asked me to marry him made me feel like I was on top of the world, that I owned the world? So, what do you do next how would you handle? What would you have done? My dopamine was through the roof. At this point I truly believed he was a doctor; however, I wasn't 100% sure if he was as rich as what he said. Whether or not, I would get that $13,000 back was debatable. But it was still difficult because I wasn't allowed to tell anyone he asked me to marry him. Now something like that, would just drive a woman crazy, don't you think it. That did put my emotions through the roof, and I just felt like the most beautiful, excited, happy person you could ever think of. Just being in this whole world or planet I never thought I'd be this happy. It was something so beautiful it was like I was a ballerina, dancing to Swan Lake, with so much grace, beauty, and clarity, so calculated, not a misstep to be had. Also, it felt like the birds that were flying high in the sky. I felt so free and graceful. It was the most exhilarating moment in my life, one I never thought I'd ever feel or have felt.

So now we were waiting from the letter from the United Nations regarding his vacation. In the first letter all it said was that he needed to be married, in my mind I thought, ok, so he will come to me and get married.

PART TWO

Well, a few more days went by, me getting even closer to him, feeling more for him, we were sexting twice a day at this point. So now what, we waited a few more days, still nothing, seemed like it took two weeks, but I received an email from the United Nations again. Stating that because the air base was under attack it was destroyed. Therefore, to get The Good Doctor, out He would have to have security because of his high standings with the United Nations., And his dedication and service that he would have to be sent to a different location, that would have a fee attached to it. Now the fee, I think it was $26,000 Canadian for him to be able to get a flight to me, obviously because of the "security measures etc.". That were attached to it. Apparently, the statue that he had with United Nations, made me a high valued member to them. Once again, here I am, freaking out, okay…like…okay, this is going to cost me money again. I had a little spat with The Good Doctor.

I would like to make a point here for you to take some time and consider how I was feeling now.

1) I had falling deeper for The Good Doctor; my phone was my soul's connection to him.

2) I was sexting with him twice a day.

3) He was sending me messages that I could feel his love radiating through the phone.

4) I felt a strong connection to him and felt his connection to me.

5) I was hooked on him.

6) I still had money in the bank.

But once again he says, listen, I don't know how this process worked, my late wife used to take care of all this, I am so sorry, I had no idea what was involved to get me to come home for a vacation. My wife took care of all that… he repeated this line several times. And the United Nations has a protocol that they must follow to do whatever was necessary to get things done. And with a bit of begging, persuading, and schmoozing, I guess you could say, he decided to talk me into it again because I did still have money in the bank, I felt at this point "I DESERVED HAPPINESS IN MY LIFE", so, I, said okay fine, I agree to pay the $26,000 to have you get flown to safety and safely to me. At this point I didn't want to see him get hurt and I really wanted to save him from all the drudgery, pain, and sorrow that he had to go through. He did display a lot of remorse of where he was, He demonstrated a lot of fear as well like a child who thought he would be beaten maimed or killed. Once again, I ended up sending a wire transfer out, as they had requested. And once that was done, he again showed all the love and support, he said he even had his bags packed ready to go, wanting to come to me it sort of felt kind of real at that point, you know. well fine, it's costing me more money, he says he's going to pay me every cent that I spent, because he said it every single time, I ended up getting a letter from the United Nations. He said, well, he's not asking for the money it's the United Nations that's asking for it and everything he said sounded logical once again, I agreed to it and did it.

Now I don't know if it was because of the amount or whatever the reason being it just seemed to take a little longer to get this process done. And taken care of. So, we did more bonding more sexting and had a couple of incidents, he was showing a lot of fear, apparently the terrorists attack and again many people were injured, hurt and he even sprained his ankle bad at one-point, dodging bombs and ammo, he was terribly upset over everything that was happening there. Now one thing that we did do a lot of was I asked him if he had something to eat. I was always concerned because he always seemed to be talking to me or working with patients or doing surgeries, so I kept asking him, did you have something to eat? And apparently because of being ransacked so many times blah blah blah that they got into the food and stole the food There was nothing to eat and that he'll just have to make do with whatever rations they give him. But he would always assure me that the military was finding ways to have more food shipped to them. The food will be there for them the next day or whatever and apparently, he ate a lot of pork and beans. That seemed to be one of the main staples that they did have available to them at the time. So, I was starting to feel worse for him, going through those issues that were happening, that just put me or at ease that I did pay the additional $26,000 to have him safely extracted from that base that he was in.

Well now it probably it took about three weeks for everything to be done and finalized for the $26,000, then, the letter stated that he had a private jet booked (just so you know that what was on the letter) with military security, to transfer him from the one base to where the plane was. (To get to the Toronto International airport) to Pearson. They even knew where he was flying to. And at least they were kind enough to say that I was going to have to be responsible to make sure nothing happened to him. "This high-ranking good doctor and his dedication service etc., "was their number one priority." The importance of his safety that it was going to be my responsibility, to make sure that he was fine and safe. The next part of the letter was what kind of shocked me again.

PART THREE

Now the second part of the letter stated the only way that they were allow The Good Doctor to come to me here in Ontario Canada was that he had to be wed. Prior to that only his wife could have him released for his vacation. As well as he did apply for retirement at the time as well. And guess what was on that letter next to that line. Yeah, you got it—the only way he could leave the base was to be married. Now to be married to him again there was a fee. Yep,

you got it, more money spent by me. Now out of love, I was willing
to pay it because I had the money in the bank for this still. So how
much was it for? But it did take a few arguments with him before
I ended up paying it. He kept saying we were connected, I was his
true soulmate, that God put us together for a reason. Sure, enough
he had the excuses, he had the reasons, he said, well like I don't
know how the United Nations works. That they have a protocol
they must follow, and they must follow it properly. The only way
to do that was to do what it says, because the United Nations only
have one way of doing things. For me, to have him here with me
would be to pay for a wedding certificate. And I said, well how are
we supposed to do that. He said, well we'd have to do it by a proxy
marriage. Wow, I've heard of it, but I never knew how a marriage
by proxy worked (naïve), yet he seemed to want to marry me still,
for some strange reason. I still wanted to marry him, so I agree to
pay money to do marriage by proxy. I felt in my heart, this must
be it the last crossroad to bare, I will finally have the love of my life
with me. I could finally get to be with someone I felt a high esteem
for, it would be an honor to be able to call my husband. Yes, I was
quite into the gentleman at this point, I consider him to be a high
valued person (myself I was feeling special, and I putting him on a
pedestal) because that's what I've been told. However, when I was
reading this letter and I was talking to him about it, the total it
was going to cost me Canadian was $60,000 approximately. Yep,
you read that correctly, $60,000. So, what does one do when one is
already spent over $13,000, another $26,000 and now, he's asked
to spend $60,000 which I had in the bank? Still. So far it wasn't
hurting me to that much, I was never a spender anyway, I've always
helped others, I didn't need anything or really want anything for
myself, but I did want The Good Doctor. He knew that about me
already. Through deliberation, communication with him and his
constant love and support that he was giving me and reminded me
of how much he has cared about me (words only) and wanted to
be with me, I wanted to be his wife. I figured okay, I'm spending

money on him instead of my children. I've already given them money and helped them out and figured maybe I should be happy too. Because he was making me feel happy. I loved how he made me feel, I felt like I was a beautiful, caring, loving person and I had the opportunity to save a very special man. Someone I've grown to really care for and start loving deeply.

After about an hour talking with him on Hangouts, I even asked him why can't we do a video chat, what would it hurt to do a video chat? Why is that an issue? If it's encrypted, anyway, how they could get into it. But again, he started in about the security measures, that they weren't allowed to do it because of the terrorists. That they would get involved with it and he could get killed. And he was trying to make me feel remorse, worry, fear. I felt lost basically. So, what does a woman do, who loves a guy endlessly and unconditionally, honestly because I was right into this gentleman, this man who was a doctor a humanitarian, who took care more about people than you can imagine.

Even stated, for about maybe the hundredth time, in our conversations that every cent that I spent I would get back, promised, and that I would even get more. Now he also said one other thing to me, but that really didn't matter because obviously money wasn't the factor for me. It's not the first time he mentioned it, but it's the first time I'm going to mention it to you. That by me paying for everything to get him out of there that I was entitled also to a $1.2 million vacation pay or spousal pay for getting him out. He also indicated the fact that it's the protocol that the United Nations uses to do what they have to do to keep the safety and process. I guess that is how to get an individual out on a UN contract.

So once again, I ended up doing my thing. I had the money in the bank anyway, I wasn't doing anything with it, was there for quite a while couple years almost, so I ended up doing another wire transfer for $60,000 to a woman in the states. (She was a liaison for the UN) same person every time that the money went to. Even though I asked him who the woman was, he said sh"s a liaison for the United Nations. So once again I ended up sending $60,000 to the woman in the United States to the bank account that she had given. I was given the information through the United Nations to send the money. I thought it was all true and valid, so that I could get married to this Good Doctor. Finally get him on a plane to me here in Ontario.

Notice how I am constantly trying to get him to me. That what they do, they make you believe that they are really coming to you, that you are finally going to have the man you love, in your arms, skin on skin so to speak.

Now if you kind of gathered i"s getting even more expensive obviously, more detailed, taking longer for it to be processed, and even waiting for the end results, whether they were going to either approve this marriage or no. (I've sent the money, they have my money now) they had all the information on me and him, (which I didn't get to see) apparently, I even asked him how did they do this? Does that get done through video chat? I thought well maybe I would at least I can meet the man that I'm supposed to be marrying? He said he didn't know the process either, he said we just must wait and see what happens.

Now during the wait as well, I was telling him that I promised myself that I was never going to get involved with another man again, because of how I was treated with mine. For the longest time in my marriage even though I was still married to him, and everybody saw it that how much love we had. (I was not happy) because I did care about him, which was confusing yet complicated at the same time. I did care for him a lot, not just I cared for him I truly grew to love him. He was infirm as well and because he was infirmed for quite a while made it difficult to think otherwise. He was so bad that we didn't even have intercourse or sexual relations the last seven years of our marriage, prior to his death. So, there were many different things going on, many different avenues and new avenues were being opened at the same time. And because I ended up telling him that he ended up telling me the fact that when his wife passed away, he promised himself that he would never remarry because she was the one for him. That she was his life, regardless of everything that had transpired and what he gone on through. So, he found out I was a devoted wife to my late husband, regardless of the circumstances and I found out he was a devoted husband to his wife. He said how much he cared and loved for her. That only made me feel closer to him more than further apart. And this does make me a little teary eyed because when you think about your emotions, your life and all the time you spent with a person you cared about, you didn't know anything else could exist or be.

PART FOUR

Now "ve got the understanding and realization of what life really is, who we are as people and what w"ve come to be. Taking that into consideration makes it difficult when you start feeling for someone different. Yo"ve never ever thought yourself to be that type of person ever in your life. It also makes you start looking at yourself in a completely different way. You start believing in life differently and looking at life differently. You start to feel alive, almost like for the first time in your whole life. Emotions play the biggest part when it comes to love, understanding and carrying as well. You start to realize what yo"ve done for the sake of love and that becomes a hard realization in you, it becomes very real, very true in your heart and in your mind. Knowing how to accept things in a different matter, in a different way, are all things that start going through your head. When someone you do"t even know gives you hope of a new beginning and a new life. And because it almost took a month prior to receiving the next letter from the United Nations, because it was a marriage by proxy, that other parties had to be involved in it. Obviously because they had to there are part to prove and then document and marry us.

In the meantime, while we were waiting, I figured okay, it's time that I start going through my husband things. That was a hard thing for me to do, when I started to do it, I had this blue lunch bag if you want to call it that, it was something that he carried with him everywhere. Inside it he kept his most prized possessions, things that meant the most thing to him. And I was sitting on the bedroom floor, I paused before I opened it because I always believed in the sanctity of trust. I believed that people had the right to have their own privacy, even if yo"re married. I do"t know if you agree or disagree with that but tha"s how I felt anyway. So here I am sitting on the floor, I opened the box and I start pulling out items that he had in it. And inside the box he would have little trinkets he loved, Coca Cola items, he had a Coca Cola marble, a Coca Cola penknife, lots, and lots of flashlights. He was like an avid believer in carrying a lot of flashlights in case one did"t work, many, plus he had so many other things little things inside his blue case. But then I came across two letters, one was addressed to me and another one also in an envelope. So, I decided to open the one that was addressed to me. I took a deep breath, now I ended up burning the letters, but "ll tell you what it said, he was explaining how much he really loved me and what I meant to him. That I meant the world to him, and he appreciated everything I did for him. He was talking about who I was and what he felt for me, none the less, also called me a nickname Foo Foo but it was spelt FU FU and at the very bottom of the letter, there was a PS, and the PS which said… the other girls meant nothing to me. While I was dumbfounded, because "ve always been faithful to my husband, I never veered off track, even though many men wanted to have me for whatever reason, I do"t know mostly because of sex I guess, but I never accepted the offers. Sadly, some of the offers came from some of his coworkers. I sat there for a few minutes', I was shocked and in disbelief, mortified I guess in a way. I never saw it, never thought once that he would do anything like that to me. The second letter that I opened was a business card, in there for when he was on a SOCO course in Toronto for a week. On the back of the card, it had the name of two girls, a room number and said come up to this room le"s have sex together. I was numb if I was angry, hurt and I felt so betrayed. And I sat there, I do"t know how long I was sitting there for, but I just seemed to be sitting on the ground, mostly in shock, I guess. And I called my brother-in-law and I told him what was in these letters, I also told Sue a friend of mine, the one thing that my brother-in-law told me, he says burn them. You do"t want to look at them anymore. And tha"s what I did, I took them outside, I sat in the chair, I put them on the ground, and I lit them on fire, watched them burn. How else does one response to something like that, really.

So then The Good Doctor ends up texting me, asking me how "m doing, whatever and I was a little slow in responding. At first my mind was still set on what he had done, never had the courage to tell me in person I guess, because he had this all in his blue box, which meant the most to him, all his prized possessions, but why keep that unless he thought it was a prize… I guess and maybe it was to him. I ended up explaining it to The Good Doctor, what I had found, He said wher"s the letters now, I said I burnt them, my brother-in-law told me to do that. And then I went from feeling hurt, to some anger because I felt I always made sure that I was pure for him and him alone. I tried to be a good Wife, do what I could for him, I guess that was"t good enough. At the time to, I guess. So, at that moment I decided or maybe even The Good Doctor might have persuaded me, I ca"t really remember, because part of was numb. In my mind really, I think anyone would feel that way if your husband had passed away almost five years prior, you find out what they did. After he passed, I ended up keeping his ashes with me, I felt like he was still with me that way. I ended up deciding that it was time to let him go. That I needed to move on, that I needed a new beginning. It kind of also helped escalate me going into the arms of The Good Doctor, my innocence was broken. I think it was the next weekend after my son and daughter-in-law who live upstairs (I live in their basement) went away for camping trip with my grandchildren. I decided to take the ashes that day to the lake because he did tell me that he wanted to be put into lake Simcoe, he had the nickname lake Simcoe frog for his CB handle, back in the old days. I guess you could say. Where his parents are buried and his grandmother and most of his relatives. I ventured my way there, talk to him the whole time, I made peace with him, I forgave him for what he did to me. Then I decided to let his ashes, go but there was also something I did"t tell you that was in his blue bin, he had a small box with rose petals in it. One of his favorite Christmas shows was, i"s a wonderful life and when he watched that the little girl Susan was sick and there was a rose next to her bed, it was dying, and she looked at her dad and she spoke. I do"t want it to die daddy, he ended up putting a couple of the Rose petals in his pocket, and said to her, if I have these road pedals, I know that yo"ll be fine. And I remember my late doing that many years ago, (I had a heart attack, he bought me roses and when they started to die, he placed some in a box) but I completely forgot about them. He said to me, if he has these rose pedals knew "ll be fine. So, when I spread his ashes into the lake, I also took the pedals and let them go with him. That way he would still have a part of me with him.

I can't tell you how long I sat alone by the lake, and who knows maybe that why I drawn to the waterfront to be close to him. Knowing that he is still with me.

Later, that day, my daughter-in-law called to ask me for something. I ca"t remember what it was, but I am I mentioned to her that I had taken Jim's ashes to lake Simcoe insert and let him go. She asked if I wasokay, I said I was fine' because I didn't about to upset anyone. The Good Doctor seems to be waiting for me, ended up texting me at some point just after I had done that. I noticed his message when I got back to the car, where my phone was. I said yes, I just say goodbye to my husband. And I said I do need some time for me right now. if you do"t mind just let me, be.

Now just going and spreading his ashes like he wanted me to be a major problem "ll explain that later. But you can see how emotions can affect an individual, just from words tha"s my point I have right now. They can either make you happy, sad, feel remorse guilt, and even shame, but they can also make you feel alive.

PART FIVE

So, when does this end, this Good Doctor kept saying to me, during our conversations over the past four months, that he was too old to start over again? He needed love in his life. But he wanted someone who did"t have baggage. And by me doing that one gesture seemed to affect him in some way that he seemed to be more emotional towards me. I ended up having to try and resolve my own feelings and accept fate of what my husband had done. I had no recourse, but just to let him know that I did love him and that I forgave him. That it was time for him to rest. I do know a part of him wanted me to always be happy and that played on me so much, I was starting to see happiness in The Good Doctor. I started to see myself with this Good Doctor. So, what did it do it transformed me into a person who had less baggage? I guess the beginning of when I started to get rid of some of my baggage. I became aware of that and knew it was time.

Now, as I had mentioned about the ashes, when I did that, and my son did"t have any knowledge of what I was doing. He started resenting me, hating me for that. He could"t accept the fact that I did this on my own, without his approval I guess you could say but emotions do take over and do many things you do"t realize. Wha"s going to happen, and you ca"t take some of them back once yo"ve done the actions. But tha"s when my son started to change his feelings towards me, I guess, when I tried to explain about the two letters, he did"t believe me, he thought I was lying, he says well wher"s the letter, so I said I burnt them.

And you could say that this was the start of the beginning of me starting to believe everything The Good Doctor was saying to me. That he was rich because he kept bringing that up to me, that he was going to pay me every cent back. That he was going to give me what I spent on him I mean. That started to change my feelings towards him in a stronger way. In a more passionate direction, I guess you could say. Having that knowledge, it started to sway me towards him more than anything else. And tha"s when I started letting go of different things. I was telling him about what was happening on Facebook, and he said you got to get off that media, i"s dangerous, the terrorist or watching. But I did"t listen to him I just left it there and just said okay whatever. Because it was my only source of communication with some of my children that are"t in the same province. I never replied on there, I just went in to see how things were. Tha"s one thing I did"t let go right away.

The Good Doctor was monopolizing most of my time at this point. He was always there, even though he was supposed to be working. Doing stuff with patients or sleeping, he just always seems to be readily available to talk to me, listen to me, the one thing I did"t realize I was doing most of the talking, I was the one expressing my feelings more so about what was happening around me, then he was. But he was so attentive to me, always tried to make me feel better about myself, that I was doing the right thing. He would say, I did nothing wrong. That I deserve some happiness in life for me, I've lived a full life already. And believe me his words made a lot of sense and up until that point he was helping me get off sleeping pills. Was always worried about what I was eating, I was trying to lose weight and I did"t eat much. For breakfast, I would have a hardboiled egg and a tea. And he kept saying you ca"t just eat an egg. I told him; I have enough fat on my body that I can do that. But The Good Doctor insisted that I should eat more than just an egg. One time he forced me to go and purchase some food like steak, potato, and salad. But The Good Doctor was very attentive to my needs. He seemed to care about me. Truthfully, I started believing The Good Doctor wholeheartedly. My feelings for him became stronger, I became amorous, and I started to have sexual feelings which amplified. Not like the sexual urges when I was with my late husband because he basically became impotent at one point, and we could"t do anything, even though I tried, I didn't know how to please him anymore That part for him just wasn't there anymore. Any sexual urges or cravings that I may have had ceased and desisted approximately 12 years ago.

As you can see, I was kind of veered into a situation that left me alone and distraught. "m sure you would understand that part. My way of thinking was way off mostly because I respect the privacy of others. I was never a jealous woman, I never veered off track, ever, I stayed pure, because I believed in the sanctity of marriage, for better or worse, sickness and in health, those words stuck to me like glue.

PART SIX

Now you will why the next part is going to make a lot of sense to you. And a lot of this is because of the dopamine level in your body. It creates happiness sadness, a lot of different things, as stated in my information page on dopamine. And your body can be your worst enemy at times, or her best friend, depending on how you look at it. But as I know now, it is those feelings I had for this Good Doctor who seemed to care deeply for me. Concerned about my well-being, my mental status, my sleep, everything. Even though it was only words that we were transporting back and forth to each other. His words affected me deep into my soul, and into my heart, my thoughts. Especially every morning, when I woke up, I would have beautiful little comments about how he felt about me. They just transcended throughout my whole body, it made me feel so good about me. I started to love myself, believe in myself, that anything is possible and Go"s here to help me.' Tha"s something we talked a lot about, was God, the belief of God. It was just like one day when I went down to the waterfront, I ended up describing what I felt and what I saw in my observation of nature and life itself.

I would tell him when I was sitting there, after a while, being alone in the quiet, the serene peacefulness around me. The water just washing down the shores, you could hear the waves beating along the shoreline. I realized that water does"t sit still, just like a human, that we always have some movement, or trace of movement within the ripples of the water. I would tell him about the trees how they represented man because the roots went deep down into the ground, where it was dark, yet the branches thrived above reaching out to the sky in the light. I said to him trees are like men because the roots see the darkness, but you ca"t see the light until you see the darkness. And I believe God created everything in duplication. This is what I told him, that everything we have here on earth has been duplicated through nature. That man reflects nature. Into man's actions, what they do what they say, how they say it" As I sat on the big rock near the end of the pier, there was a little field mouse, it kind of came out from a corner of a rock, took one look at me, and then darted away. I said to him wow, tha"s just like a human, what they do"t understand they fear and run. I kept telling him that I was"t a normal woman, that the way I think is way beyond other women for the most part. That I looked at life differently and how much I love nature, observing it, mesmerized by it enchanted beauty because God created all this for us. I said to him the sad part is when I watched humans doing their things during the day, they do"t stop to smell the roses. Unfortunately,

In my defense i"s not that "m trying to justify anything tha"s happened or what transpired after this point. "m just trying to let you know, how your feelings can really get in the way of seeing the light. I"s not till you find out how bad the darkness is. You must forge forward, have faith in yourself, believe in yourself to overcome the obstacles.

So now you know why I started believing in The Good Doctor. In a way, but I will explain how it all transpires near the end. That you can understand and what you need to look for to help you judge yourself, because I do"t believe in judging people, I know we all judge ourselves and w"re our worst enemy quite honestly.

PART SEVEN

We must look forward to things that create reality. It's what we have now that matters.

It took quite a while to find out about this proxy by marriage, I think it was almost a month. One of the reasons I told you about my husband and his ashes was because when I got home later that evening. I was coming to terms with what I had done. What I had said to him, forgave him, told him I loved him and will always have a place in my heart for him. Another week went by, The Good Doctor and I were getting even closer, or I was getting closer to the doctor mentally and emotionally. As well as physically because le"s face it he turned me on. His words were getting to me.

But I opened my email it was (about a week later after I put my late husband to rest.) and it was"t really a surprise because I did pay the $60,000 for this proxy, I see this marriage certificate, and it had said that I was wed to The Good Doctor and congratulated us on our marriage. The thing that put me on my keester was the fact that the day we were apparently where wed., It just so happened to be the day that I released my husband and put him to rest July 1²¹h, 2021. That kind of left me emotional, as I think it would to any one of you. I never would have thought that the day I decided to put my husband to rest was the day I apparently was married to another man. That affects your dopamine levels to a high extreme. (On a bad note, that is). However, how can one feel happy on the very same day. I relayed the information to The Good Doctor, and he said he had already received a copy of the wedding certificate. I said I thought one of us would have at least had to have been there for this, marriage by proxy. And I guess that was the start of the end for me, because tha"s when things started to get rocky between the two of us. A little bit. He did"t think anything of it, the fact that the day I put my husband to rest was the day that we were married.

Where do I go from here, well let me tell you what happened next, because I think i"s important for you to know. What happened to me so that it might leave an impact with you. That it may save you from grief, pain, sorrow, humiliation, and feeling like a fool. You see a narcissist works in many ways but the one thing they are is consistent. They keep trying to make you feel good about you, regardless of the situation or the outcomes. And above all they try to show you that you deserve happiness, that God put you together for a reason, and that everything you do is pre planned by God.

Now le"s get on to the next part we ended up with, the marriage by proxy, that was it for me. That day no other information from them. At point, but then we received the letter from the

United nation or an email really, I call them letters sometimes sorry about that I guess i''s my old school. But to carry on, I ended up with an additional letter from the United Nations, stating now to let the distinguished Good Doctor who is valued tremendously by the United Nations, for his service and all his efforts to be released into my custody. I would have to pay an additional, I think it was almost $205,000. Yes, you read that right, $205,000. Which was more than I had. I did not have enough money in the bank for it, nor could afford, to get a loan or whatever for it. I have no value left. The previous year I sold my house to my daughter undervalued. (Way below market value because tha''s all she could afford.) Now I think you know where this is going. it gets worse, and this is where his manipulation starts to come out threefold. You see I only had maybe $60,000, left in my bank account. I had given the rest to my children, Like I said ''m not a very materialistic person at all. Items, things. Prestige. Where never part of me. I just wanted to help my children and just have enough so that I had a little nest egg in case I ever needed it. So, you want to know where this all went, well I hope yo''re sitting down because yo''re going to find out.

When I was talking to The Good Doctor it became a very heated discussion. I told him that there was no way I could come up with $205,000 Canadian dollars. That I was unable to do that, my situation and what has transpired over the past year. He says oh you must have something, you can sell paintings, jewelry, something, property. Now through our other heated discussions that we did have in the past I did tell him that I owned a house, but I sold it way under value. That I help my children out and in essence gave over $500,000 away in total. I told him again I was''t a materialistic type of person, items mean nothing to me. He said money is only paper, it does''t have any meaning, you can find a way to get this money. Well, the argument got worse, at one point I blocked him on my Facebook and on Hangouts. Then The Good

Doctor decided to email me, which I forgot about altogether. I did"t know how to block it anyway so my bad. I guess because tha"s where things really went bad.

Now he ca"t communicate with me, and I had called him everything in the book at this point, on Hangouts. And thought okay i"s over. "m done, I ca"t do anymore, "ve only got $60,000 left I love this man, however, if it has it be, tha"s as far as it goes. He got over $200,000 off me already, wha"s another $200,000 according to him. But he kept begging me and begging me and begging me to come back to talk with him. That we can resolve this issue. And like a fool or a lost little puppy, I ended up putting him back in Hangouts again. And we started communicating again, during this communication, I tried to go things to resolves what we had available to us. What was needed. He kept saying read over the contract, what are they asking for. Not giving me any answers, (you see, he wanted me to find a way to make it less, his manipulation path) he wanted me to figure it out myself, on how to deal with this process. And yes, according to him, its protocol, a process that the United Nations goes through to keep the sanctity and safety of their high valued officials safe and secure. I know that is repetitive sorry, but that line was text to me too many times I lost count, So I read it again and what It said was it was, going to cost I proximately $95,000 for his consignment box, which included all is information on his banking (something he said to me) all his information on him, he had like six or seven medals in there that he had received because of what are you done. And the process to get the $1.2 million that apparently was owed to me as his spouse. The second part of the letter stated that he was in arrears for taxes and that for him to be cleared, the taxes had to be paid. Now that part there was $200,000. So now yo"re looking at $295,000, that the United Nations wanted me to give them, they said, I was responsible for because I was his legal wife, that I had to come up with this money, when a I was"t working, I was on a wido"s pension, my money is almost all depleted in my bank.

I told him he had to try and write a letter to the United Nations, explaining the situation that there was no way I was able to come up with this money. We kind of agreed to that we both write letters (I was the only one doing the writing, he just wanted me to think he was doing it at the time.) to the United Nations to try and resolve this issue. I said maybe they can take the money off him or take it off what "m supposed to get. to clear up whatever issues he has with the United nation. He did state to me that his wife always paid everything up for him (ii told him she had access to his money, she didn't have to worry or make the money herself), again, that he didn't know the process, that she knew what was involved and what needed to be done, to resolve or get him to come home on leave. And he was quite adamant about that, played very innocent about it the whole time. I know in my emails to the United Nations, we're all about trying to find a way to resolve the issues so that he can leave the war zone. He said that he was writing letters as well, however, I never seen any of his letters, (yet he wanted to see mine) that he had written (so that that could just be words and most likely it was just words nothing more, nothing less). At least that's what I think, This went on for a couple of weeks and he kept saying to me read the letter over again, read what they're asking for. I had no clue what he wanted me to discover in those words from the United Nations. But then once again because he coerced me to look at the situation in a different perspective. Answer, once again I looked at it and it was like it jumped out at me. Well, if we can get the consignment box, then I should be able to have access to your money correct. (This is exactly what he wanted me to find, yes, his manipulative patience worked) he said yes. I guess he put a smile on his face that day when I said that to him, huh? So anyway, I said there is a problem, still. I only have about $60,000 left in the bank, we need over $90,000 to get you or get me to the point where I could get the consignment box. I said, well write up a letter to the United Nations asking that if we do that, will that be sufficient for me to get the consignment box, so that I can access your banking information and pay off your debt. He agreed to write a letter and I did as well to state what we wanted to do. As it all went on, we waited to see if we could get a reply. now we got a reply from the banister of the UN, stating that the consignment box would cost was just a little over ($90,000 and The Good Doctor gave the amount Canadian, he always did all the calculations by the way) obviously and instructions on how to send the monies. Which was again by a wire transfer to the woman in the US. Now up on that statement, I assumed, and I confirmed it with The Good Doctor, that it sounds like they're approving the fact that they will send me the consignment box, so that I can access his funds to pay off the difference for him to leave the war zone.

So now I'm stuck with the proposition that was handed to us (me). I only had $60,000 but I needed an additional $30,000 plus to get the amount necessary to get the consignment box. How does one who has nothing accomplish that? What does one do, I discussed this in very deep detail with The Good Doctor? So now I'm biting at the bit to figure out how we (me) going to get the rest of the funds necessary to get the consignment box, and him be able to leave the war zone. So, The Good Doctor and I tried to figure out different ways, (he kept saying things that I thought were off the wall) he was trying to say, do this, do that, uh sell your jewelry, sell paintings, you've got money, don't you have property somewhere you can sell keep, saying that a lot to me. But I don't think he ever listened to what I wrote or put it between the eyeballs or whatever (all he was thinking of is how is he going to get the money from me?) you want to call it, because to no avail I kept telling him that I had nothing. I had no collateral at all I had was a vehicle in my name. Then he said to me, well can't you get a loan for that amount? Well, I could try and get a loan, but I said to them there's no way they're going to loan me that much money. I have nothing left my bank accounts almost depleted, I've only got a widow's pension as all I've been living off because I had money in the bank. I didn't have to worry about money really. So how do I get this money and after he pushed and persuaded, I decided okay fine I'm going to try and go for a loan.

The next day I decided to go over to the bank and see if I could make an appointment for a loan. And with COVID and everything else it had to be done by appointment only, so I booked the date in to go and see the bank representative, which was the following week at some point. In the meantime, once again he's pulling at my heartstrings, sexting me telling how much he loves me and that we were meant to be together, that we were soulmates, that it's true love, that he never felt anything like this for any other woman but me. He knew of all the work I've put in and that I was able to move mountains. So, when the great day came, I ended up going to the bank, sitting down with the with the bank advisor. I asked him if I could get a loan for $60,000, he said because of my income and I don't have any collateral which I knew was going to happen anyway, (I figured he was going to turn me down) but instead he gave me a loan for $9500, that would help somewhat it was a line of credit. So, then I had to formulate okay, what am I going to do next. (Now in my mind I was thinking I was getting the consignment box) how am I going to get a some more money. The Good Doctor was happy that I got approved for something, but he said you could do better. So, then I went to a shark place that charges an arm and a leg like 50% more interest than anywhere else just to see if I could get one there. I didn't want the one showing up and not being able to get more money. So, I went there and was given a loan for $9,000. So that was $18,500 that I needed towards goal. I was short some more money and I'm thinking okay, no other bank's going to give me any more money. What am I going to, then I realized, okay, I have credit cards, which some of them I never have used and they have lines of credits on them, as well at higher rate mind you, but so I did that and I managed to scrape up enough money almost not quite enough money with the shy of $2,000. And then I did something, only because I believed that he was going to come to me and that this was going to settle the whole thing. And I asked my one friend if she could loan me $2,000 to make up the difference, I needed to get. This in turn took me about a week and a half to do to try and raise that money. He was ecstatic, he was happy, The Good Doctor felt oh my gosh you can move mountains you're amazing with what you can do.

It was like an adrenaline rush, or the dopamine was working well. Because now that I was able to raise enough money for his consignment box, with the way the banister gave us the information it sounded like they had approved the process, that what we had chosen' (what I had done) being the only option. And again, The Good Doctor said, don't worry every cent you spent you will get paid back threefold don't worry about it, I got your back, when I get there, you're going to get your money. So, then what does one do we ended up celebrating, he became very amorous because I was able to raise enough money for the consignment box. I said to him, I said I just hope they approve everything the way we anticipated it, because there's no way I'll be able to come up with any more money. He told me once I get the box that I will be able to get access and pay off his debt. He assured me that everything will be fine, that the banister will do everything he possibly could to assist and aid him. He is prestigious doctor for the UN on a military mission have humanity.

Once again, we waited and waited and waited, it almost seemed like each time it took longer to do the process. And in the meantime, he got closer and closer and closer in my heart. There were times I got really antsy about it. What's going on what's taking so long. (I now had debts to pay because it) He kept saying well it's the process, it's the way they do things, its protocol, we can't judge what they do we just have to let them do their thing. Just wait for them to reply. Eventually I think about 2 1/2 weeks after they ended up sending a letter. I get an email stating that they got the money for the consignment box but cannot ship it out to me because of the taxes owed by The Good Doctor. And I said to The Good Doctor, well, you told me that this would work. He says I can't judge what they do, I'm not the United Nations, I must do what they say. To me it almost seemed like he didn't have a backbone to stand up for himself or any of his rights or whatever. And I just said to him, there's no way I can come up with that kind of money. As it was, I ended up having to go through a lot just to get the difference for the box. 8i couldn't get $200,000 from anywhere. long story short I did try even went on the dark web, to get the money but I was unable to do it. He said that they owed him over $12 million. Which I don't know if that was real or whatever, but I doubt it now, but at the time I did believe him. So, what does one do now? How can one process anything. So for the next week or two we ended up both emailing the United Nations and the banister for a plea to either use the money I was supposed to get or money from him rob Peter to pay Paul basically, to cover his expenses that they wanted paid and every time we tried calling or emailing, I wasn't getting any responses he was getting the odd ones apparently, funny that I wouldn't get them because I was the one paying the money. I didn't think of that at the time quite honestly. What is the next step how do we get past this now, quickly but it was too hasty in my report because I was going to be stuck with the bills?

In the meantime, he wanted me to try and find a way to get the other $200,000 necessary to pay his taxes. So then I decided to go underground and see if I can find a place that would loan me $200,000 in one shot to pay the bill I read it so I did a lot of Internet research not research looking up places that gave money away on the Internet and helped people out, I called a place up when I said I need a loan, well I had to fill out a form online and said that I needed $200,000, they had checked out my application and said yeah we can handle that for you ....which kind of shocked me. And then the guy said, but it's going to cost you must pay the insurance upfront on the loan. And I said, well what's that going to cost me and that was $9,000. So then now I must figure out a way to get $9,000 how does one get $9,000. So, I ended up going to another underground company for a loan for $9,000 but ended up with $8,000 in a loan yet another loan. So, then I scrounge and got some money to make up the difference it took a while for me to get it but a couple weeks later I had the full amount. And when I ended up sending the money to the gentleman, he said that's perfect will process everything and get that money to you right away. And they said it was supposed to be in within the same day of receiving the remainder of the money. Nothing was done that day so later on the next day when nothing still happened, I ended up calling them and saying how come I haven't got the money yet, the guy was surprised, he says you haven't got it yet! I said no, so then he ended up checking on it and giving me a call back. Telling me that they ended up giving the loan to somebody else because I took too long. They didn't tell me there was a criterion time to get it done. But then he came back with a response that they could give me another loan with an offshore banker an undisclosed individual, I guess, for $300,000. And I said I only needed $200,000. And he said, well it's for $300,000 we can guarantee it for you 100%, I knew it was going to be a cost more, to this and he said, well you'll need another $9,000. Well, this is getting harder and harder for me to do and trying to rack up this money that's not going to be easy. I ended up making up to $14,500, that I paid this company, and I just couldn't seem to find any other way. At the time to get that fund I asked my daughter for help, and I found out that the company wasn't real, that I was being conned by then. Which now is being investigated by the police department as well.

Apparently, they were being unethical too with how they were obtaining cash for signing up for loans. Still haven't heard back and I did not receive my $14,500 back from that company. So, I was stuck at square one. I had no way of getting that $200,000 at this point because everything I did, I tried to do out of love for this man. Because I was truly in love with him at the time. Then he said, sell stuff, sell whatever you can, let's start little that bits, little bits so I ended up going to Toronto one Friday (I was angry with them, with The Good Doctor, everyone, I wanted to just leave, and most of all I was angry at myself. I knew at this point I was being played) and my children ended up calling the police on me. I just left and didn't tell them where I was going. I didn't think that was a criterion for me to do. I thought I was old enough to take care of myself. And they ended up calling every police department across Canada. So, it got quite complicate, I wasn't even away for 9 hours and I ended up with a phone call from the OPP, then I ended up with a policeman at my door, when I was trying to fall asleep, at 11:30 at night. And then I received another phone call around midnight from the police department. Apparently, my children told them that I was suicidal, that I forgot my pills, that I wasn't taking my pills and all kinds of different things to get the police department to search for me. They could see that everything was fine with me, where I was, I was by myself in a hotel room in Toronto. Even The Good Doctor didn't hear from me and sent me an email.

In the meantime, while I was away my daughter-in-law, they ended up searching my apartment and found information about The Good Doctor in detail., some information (I wrote some of it down because I was trying to reach goals and how much I needed to get) (everything else like this so the paperwork was all in the drawer). I kind of felt violated in a way, at the time however I was kind of glad too. Even though I was in Toronto, I wanted to solve and stop all what was going on. It was getting harder and harder for me to do anything, to help The Good Doctor. I even told The Good Doctor give up on me, give up the queen, go somewhere else find yourself another queen.' I can't do this anymore for you. I said I can't do it at all, I was done. I didn't even talk to him the one night I was at the hotel, He ended up emailing me again, because I wasn't responding to his Hangouts. I told him that the police were there. And that my children were fully aware of what was going on. It didn't seem to bother him at the time. He said everything will be fine, don't worry about it, once I get there everything will be fine. just find a way to get that $200,000 (in your dreams). Sell a property he says again, I have no property, I already told him that. if I had property, I would have had money. To him it seemed like it was becoming the almighty dollar.

PART NINE

In the process I have questioned him many times, why can't he access his funds. He said because it's so secure there that they're not allowed to use the Internet for their banking information. He gave me all kinds of excuses of how he couldn't get the money, or how he wishes I would get the money. I even said to him because I was trying to divert him (I said I had a chance of getting the money) and see what he was really made of, I said, well, do you want me to go to the bikers (place my life at risk) and see if I can get money from them, just for you, to save you. I said it would be dangerous, but I would do it for you I came close to doing that too, but then I realize this isn't right. Then there was an intervention here at the house, when the police ended up showing up, my daughter and one of my best, old friends where the police were there, my daughter had flowers for me.

And that's when the police were talking to me, whatever about what was going on with this guy that I've been talking to online. I ended up telling them the truth, that I had already given him more than $200,000 and they instinctively called it a major crime. What was I going to do now? I'm married to the gentleman. I even showed the police my phone where I had the marriage certificate. The officer looked at that the certificate and said it's a fake. I said you can tell just by looking at it! He says yeah, I've seen a lot of my day. So here I am penniless, thinking I was married, when I wasn't, to a man that I thought loved me, (this is when all my doubts were finally answered) but only found out he was in the love for money. What does one do at this point? How can one considering what's happened expect to move forward?

PART TEN

I did tell him that I wasn't a normal woman normal thinking woman, I ended up confronting him and telling him that the marriage certificate was fake. That he was a con, he was using me, his name wasn't The Good Doctor, I'll say. That he wasn't who he said he was, that I didn't believe it was his picture. He kept saying, listen, don't talk to and don't trust third parties, they're all lying to you, they're terrorists…they're trying to stop us from being together. (I KNEW THAT THE POLICE WOULDN'T LIE TO ME.) You and I were meant to be together, you're my true love. I'm yours, its fate. Well it was kind of hard not to talk to him, but I also wanted to find out the reasoning behind all this. I wanted answers. He didn't know that the police showed up here at the time. He didn't know that I went to the police station and wrote a report. Gave them all the information I had on my phone, which I could access. But no sooner did I get the information to the police department, that The Good Doctor ended up texting me and saying how dare you involve the police in our relationship. Are you having affair with the police officer the man handling your case? In my defense it was a female police officer, I'm not into females okay. I'm sorry to say this but, I don't do females. I was only a one-man woman to start with.' because I've only had one man in my whole life. We had fights and whatever and he was still trying to sway me to get the money to save him, so he can come to me and prove to everyone that he was who he said he was.

It did get to a point where I didn't speak with him anymore. and When I stopped all communication with him, strange things were happening on my phone. I ended up blocking him on Hangouts. He figured out a way to get back into my phone. Ended up leaving messages somehow, via other people I had in my phone. He called me an Internet trollop, a Jezebel, but before I tell you what happened next I just need to back up for a minute and explain something else that happened.

Now as soon as the police got involved with this case, now I was completely broke, had no funds or money at all. I was just my pension that I Get monthly. But what happened next really shocked me more than anything else. It hurt a lot. My children decided that they were going to have my account frozen. They thought I was insane. Because of how I was with this gentleman over the Internet. I will say most of the changes I made were for my betterment. I guess they differed what that information was to me. Now my account is frozen, I have no access to any money. When I went to go use my card. (That was the way I found out that I had no use or access to the funds) in my account. I said, well, what if I need to buy food or gas. The bank informed me that I had to wait until they finish their investigation, prior to releasing my funds back to you. At this point I didn't know that my children were the ones that were behind this. Every day I would call and say have you unfrozen my account. I would scrounge for change in the house, just to get milk or whatever I needed, like food wise mostly eggs, because they were cheap. Funny thing though, is the two that did live in Ontario with me (the ones that tried to deem me insane) here didn't, even offer me a dime or see if I needed anything, to help me out whatsoever.

Because I gave them a lot of money, prior to this happening, they still treated me like I was a piece of scum. That and because I didn't have money, they had no use for me. My son and daughter-in-law wanted to kick me out of their apartment twice. (Since then. and now this was the third time, at the end of this month I did not have a place to live. I didn't have a place to go really of my own) and at the end of this month I had to be out. Plus, I didn't want to be somewhere I wasn't wanted, I must be out of this apartment. One reason is because I want someone in my life for me, just like they have someone in their lives. I ended up going on a date with a guy, he had too much to drink, he had a long drive back home on a motorcycle, so I ended up letting him sleep on my couch that night. My son was very upset the fact that I had a strange man sleeping on the couch. One of their excuses was COVID, but I knew he didn't have that. He wasn't even near any of them anyway, it's a complete separate unit from theirs. But I think it was my son, because he was upset that I had some man sleeping where I live.

My son also started not talking to me. Whatsoever he told me that to him I was dead, that two is to my grandkids I no longer existed to them. These were words, he said to me very hurtful, very painful, and I didn't know what to say or do. My daughter-in-law said it was son, because he was upset about the fact that I got rid of his dad's ashes without letting him know. (or partake in it in any shape or form) I did tell him this the one thing, is that Jim wanted me to do that alone. What does one do, how does one cope with something like this? I was distraught, I was hurt, I was mortified So I just keep going for my daily walks keeping to myself calm, trying to stay clear of my grandkids, who I adore and would do anything for. Just like I would have done anything for my son, daughter-in-law, my daughter, my other son in law, my other daughter, my other son in law, and all my grandkids. The one thing they always knew was they could count on me when they needed help. They were portraying themselves as victims, not saying that I was a victim in this at all. The coping factors of this is very difficult mortifying and many other things that right now just blow my mind.

As all this was going on The Good Doctor was still trying to contact me, still trying to stay in communications. He says they don't have any right treating me the way they did. I was still talking to him because I wanted to find out who he was. I wanted to give as much information and leverage to the police that I possibly help them with. At this point because of my inquisitive nature, I needed to know. I had to know where he was, who he was, why he did this to me, most of all how he did this to me, it was a mystery to me. I was always the type of person who is pretty good with their money. I never had to worry about money. suddenly now my life has turned upside down. what's going to happen next, how am I going to survive. And he kept insisting that they were all lying, that the devil was at work. He was trying to tell me that he is who he is. He kept saying he loved me dearly, kept sending me morning messages, every morning trying to get my heart completely back to him.

Now as now as the investigation was continuing and police department were starting to assemble a process of what needed to be done. They had informed me that the marriage certificate was 100% fake. And that the money I sent to the states too United States to the one woman there they ended up having a trooper go to her place and she denied everything. But the one thing I could not understand is the trooper ended up giving her a copy of one of the wire transfers, that was sent to her. This had my phone number and all my information on there. After the trooper left, she called me up, she ended up calling up the guy that she sent the money to who, was in a different country altogether, the Netherlands. He told her we'll call her up, she was the one that did it, she approved all this. That she knows everything that's going on. The woman called me up and started talking to me on the phone. We were having a hard time hearing each other, so she asked if I was on Facebook, became a friend and we ended up doing a video chat together (that's where I found out about where the money was sent, to who, and that she didn't work for the United Nations). Talk about a crazy situation right… she didn't know who the person was, this so-called Good Doctor. All she knew was that the money was sent to her and she had to send it off to this one guy that she knew, She never really met him, but seen him on FaceTime and that they became friends, Now in the meantime, I was still talking with The Good Doctor as well, because he was just chomping at the bit to find out anything he possibly could. I guess plus he was also still trying to persuade me to raise that money for him. When I told him that part about the woman in the United States, He insisted that she did work for United Nations. That she had to go under secrecy because on the severity of the matter that he was a diplomat, under cover for the United Nations. Every time I said something to him, he said it's a lie, they're telling you a lie. I told him that I video chatted with the woman, and she denied everything. She said to me, I have people in the military, and they don't pay taxes for starters, it doesn't cost them. She seemed a little baffled and confused as to what The Good Doctor had told me. I explained some of the information he had sent to me. And yet he had an excuse It didn't matter whenever I brought money up, or why he couldn't get it himself or whatever the case may be, it was at first that he didn't have access because of the Internet, that his information would be compromised, and he could be killed because of it. At one point he told me that the reason why he couldn't access his funds was because the United Nations was taking care of all his property and everything else and his two expensive cars.

PART ELEVEN

So basically, as we were talking, I kind of calmed down a little bit, (just because I wanted to get more information off him,) I wanted to play him now and con him if I could. So, for about a week I was communicating with him, suddenly, I get a message from him on Facebook. I go, this is odd, what's going on here? He sent a message that said, hi Susan how are you I said why are you on here, you're not supposed to be on here. No response, I thought ok, I haven't talked to him on Hangouts he trying to get me to talk here. Someone else was on there, which I thought was him. It didn't take long for him to admit he wasn't The Good Doctor to me. He said it wasn't, at this point here I was questioning everything. Now the person that was on Facebook wasn't speaking the same way that The Good Doctor spoke to me. it was a broken English, which also confused me. I thought maybe he was using word translator, so that the words came out in very good English. And that was one of the reasons why he ended up choosing hang out. Just so I couldn't see that it there was a translator involved. But as it went on, I said why are you here. He says I needed to talk to you.,' because I want your picture and I said you have my pictures. I've sent you pictures, and he said send pictures now. So, I complied because I was trying to figure out what was going on, sent him some pictures. And then he said pictures of my boobs, I want to see your ***** boobs. I thought that was quite odd honestly, that that's what he wanted to see a picture of. I didn't comply with that, I just sent him a few more pictures of me. And then I said to him are you okay, what's wrong, did something happen to Hangouts? And I said, I was really worried about him and said I love you, but I need to know the truth. I said a couple nice things about what I thought of him, from the person that I had originally associated with. After all being a humanitarian, helping people, saving lives, risking himself for the life of humanity. And then the person said to me you speak so well. You talk beautifully. I said, well thank you. I believe that communication is one of the biggest parts of any person's persona. That you need to speak properly to talk to anyone.

And while I was talking to him all sudden.

I get a message from The Good Doctor on Hangouts. So, I went over to Hangouts, I said okay, you're here now, any question why I said it that way. I said to him, well I was just talking to you on Facebook, and he says I'm not on Facebook. I stopped using Facebook a long time ago. It wasn't safe, it was an insecure program. And I said, well who's using your name on Facebook? So, then he left for a few minutes and came back then questioned me, I thought you stopped using Facebook, well not 100% I said. I still have my children on there that I need to communicate with. And he got upset with me. The fact that I was talking to this gentleman on Facebook using his profile. And he said he's a terrorist… he said don't you Remember Me telling you that. We were ambushed and the terrorists got in, they stole my computer. They have my information. It was funny though, every time I did ask him a question about something, he always seemed to have a response to it. He always had a way to make things look like it was so believable that you can just understand exactly what he's going through. But at what point does a lie end and the truth start is my question. I guess what I'm trying to say is that things did not just add up properly. I was just only finding more lies, upon lies, to be honest. But I said okay, fine, I'll stop using Facebook (once again, I didn't tell him that I was still on Facebook quite honestly because I still wanted to talk to the individual that was using his name on Facebook). I wanted to see where this was going, why this was happening, who these people really, how many were involved, was he a part of it or just a Patsy, to it who knows because I never got that answer.

Chapter Nine

THE RED HERRING

So, I just made it seem like the old days, with The Good Doctor. That I could still be in communication with him, get as much information and data that I could. To submit to the police department. In the meantime, I was communicating (for about a week) with someone using his website on Facebook. (Knew it wasn't The Good Doctor because I was getting messages from both at the same time) We had a nice long chat for couple of days, the first time we talked, he kept saying how beautiful I was. The way I spoke was perfectly beautiful, and the way I described things to him was amazing. Not that I don't think I speak any different than any of anyone else but knowing how important it is, just to make sure that I get the point account across properly, which is something I always valued. And then he said to me, well, I'm tired now, I need to go to sleep. He ended up saying it like "fed me sleep". So, it was really broken up English. Before he went to sleep, he said to me, "I love you", still pretending like it was the real doctor. I said I love you too have a good sleep, to keep up the façade, we'll talk tomorrow. Then he says can I have a kiss before I go to sleep? So, I sent him a little imago kiss. He sent me a teddy bear hug with hearts, image, lying in bed sleeping. Now the next morning he was already on Facebook. While the real Good Doctor was on Hangouts, (at the same time) they're both texting at the same time, Typing simultaneously. I started questioning the one on Facebook about who he was really. Tell me about yourself because I know you're not The Good Doctor. And during our conversation, he did admit that he was not a Good Doctor at all. He was in fact a completely different person; he gave me a name which I can't even pronounce quite honestly and that he lived in India. And I said, well can I see a picture of you? He said why do you need this picture? I'm just curious as to what you look like. I said, well how old are you? He didn't answer. Then I tried to use my persuasion, my words to make him feel better about himself, so that I could access more information from him. And eventually he did tell me that he was 25 years old. He lived in India and was going to school. I asked him why did you take my money? You took everything I had. He said he was sorry, I said, well if you're sorry, why don't you just give me my money back. No response. So, then I asked him what are you taking in school? Then he started saying, "we make good love, you make good love we have love, I come we have love". I said, yes, I am good in bed, I can please any man, because of all the experience I've had over the years. That just intrigued him, he just loved that line and wanted more from me. Now, I wasn't sure how it was going to handle this part, but I did not have any sexting with him okay…. just so you know. He was younger than my oldest grandson. I don't roll that way. But anyway, he ended up telling me that he was not The Good Doctor. He called him (The Good Doctor) priest at first then the doctor. I kept trying to get more and more information off him, maybe about The Good Doctor, it seemed like he knew the doctor in a way. Maybe the doctor was giving him a course on something. He also mentioned what type of schooling he was in, but I didn't understand what it was, because he expresses it in his language, then said he was studying for an exam. Said, I'll let you go so you can study; we can talk another time. He goes more pictures please. I sent him a couple of more pictures, clothed obviously and he goes no no no and I said yes yes yes, that's all you're getting right now. So, I said goodnight to him and good luck on his exam.

On the flip side The Good Doctor believing that I'm back on his side, thinking, I have chosen him over the police department, (and all the evidence that says everything that he said to me was false and misleading) A CON IN FACT. But I ended up talking with him, trying to get information off him by asking him certain questions, about the United Nations, how it worked, how he got there? I tried to get information about his wife, but none of that, I was able to get a straight answer from him. But I had to do it in a way that he didn't realize that I was just trying to find out more information about him. I did ask him, isn't it possible for you to video chat so that I can see who I'm talking with to prove that you are who you are. I know it wasn't the first time I asked him, but I also knew that he wasn't going to do it for me, I knew he didn't have a backbone and that he was a con.

I'm starting to believe that he was a con. Nothing more, because he didn't care about me, all he cared about was the money. That was a sad part really, I had a tremendous number of feelings for this man, and I couldn't let him go without letting him know how he made me feel. I was pulling at straws at this point. I wasn't sure how I was going to take it mentally, as well as physically. I knew I wasn't a normal thinking woman, but I didn't know how much it was going to affect me, I've always tried to keep my emotions in check. It was the emotions that always seemed to cause the issues for many people, I was aware of that over the years, by just watching others and observing others. So basically, I just kept talking to him for a few more days.

As per the one on Facebook he ended up telling me that he wasn't the doctor, he apologized for that. I told him that I was being conned by that man who called himself a doctor. He goes may help you. I couldn't understand how or what that meant. I said okay, how can you help me, but he didn't respond. No matter how many ways I asked the question no response. So, then I asked him how did your exam go? He said not good, I think. Well, I said I'm sorry to hear that, but I know you can make it if you put your effort into it. He said you are beautiful woman, I love you. I said, I love you too sweetheart but I'm old I'm 63 years old and I'm way too old for you. You're younger than my oldest grandson. He says I come to you, I said sure… get on a plane you can come to me, and I will love you. He says if I got on a plane to come, would I want him? I set of course, come to me and I'll prove it to you. (In honesty all I wanted to catch the con) No response, we ended up talking for a few days.

In the meantime, The Good Doctor was going on his other computer, I guess, checking out Facebook and found out that he was online with me. Prior to that, he kept saying do I have a certain app on my phone so that we could talk because his phone was dying. At that time, I had my forgotten my password for my apple app, so I ended up having to wait for a new password. The one; laying the part of The Good Doctor on Facebook wanted me to go into WhatsApp. He wanted to talk to me there. But we did talk again a little bit longer. I didn't find any more information that was useful, that would help me out, but he said we can't be here no more. It not safe. I still want to talk to him, and he complied he stayed on for a couple more days.

Now The Good Doctor did not tell me that he's been trying to figure out who was on his Facebook account, and what I was doing on there, I was treated things as normal, I wasn't about to disclose any other information to him on that fact. He was sending me still the most beautiful morning messages on how much he adores and loves me. How much nature is correlated with the soul of life and serenity. He told me how much I mean to him, that I was his world. The only one he could count on, love and want to be with for the rest of his life. But if I ended up asking him any personal questions, he'd just evade it and wait for me to say something else. Like, I love you or whatever the case may be, but at this point here I was only saying the words. Starting not to feel anything at this point. As I was numb from everything that I found out that it was really hurting me inside.

Then I get another call from the woman in the United States. She wanted to talk to me some more, for some reason I think she was now trying to get information out of me, to see what I knew so, that she could relay the message back to The Good Doctor. Whatever else that needed to know of what was going on and what has transpired through the investigation. So here I am, stuck in a threesome type of conversations, I guess, because all of these people that were technically involved in the same con, I would imagine.

I guess you can say I wasn't a normal individual to start with. Who else would sit there and still talk to someone that you knew conned you? Someone that was using someone else's Facebook account, who was the second individual. And the third person who ended up accepting money… you would think if someone accepted money of that caliber, that they'd start questioning what it's for or something. Instead of just handing over money without any foreknowledge of what it was for. You can bet she was getting money to do these transfers. in a sense they were just laundering money if you ask me. So, you can see that it just gets more and more complicated as the time goes on. Unfortunately, it just becomes a bigger picture in the end. tired I'm cold I want to go home

Chapter Ten

SAYING GOODBYE

The girl from Texas United States, and yes, I did ask The Good Doctor on several occasions who is the person that I'm sending the money to. He kept saying it was a liaison for the United Nations and that's part of their procedure, how their protocol worked. that's how they must follow path. Always having answers for everything and very quickly too may I add. But another few days passed, the more information I was finding out about The Good Doctor, the more I could see that what he was saying and what I was being told was obviously, two completely different things. It got to a point where I started accusing him about being a con mostly because I knew and wasn't going to get any further than this with him. I was done with him. He cheated me out of my money, robbed me blind, but knew in my heart that I would never get my money back from this con man.

He then said something funny, because he always called me babe unless he was getting upset with me. He would call me Sue and he goes listen, so I'm telling you the truth, it's not me, it's all of them, they're lying, they're terrorists, they don't want us to be together. What would be the sole purpose of keeping two people apart is what I don't understand. Where do I go from here, what can I do, how can I do it, I ended up telling him point blank that he was a liar. Then he started to get his pants in or Knot. I guess you could say and said to me, I love you, we're soulmates, its fate, we were meant to be together, God wanted us together, you've seen it in your dreams, I've seen it in my dreams, we belong together, you're my true love and I'm your true love. That's all it should matter, we should be happy together, once I'm out of here, I will take you away from all that. I'll prove to everyone that I am a real person. He was using all he could to try and persuade me.

That he was the real thing and when I said what's your name, what's your real name? He got very perturbed and angry with me. When I tried to say that he wasn't The Good Doctor, who he was? He said, well why would you even ask me a question like, that you know my name, tell me my name, he basically said in a very harsh manner. *He kept pushing and pushing me, so I finally said you're The Good Doctor. He said that's right don't forget it. You're my wife, you're supposed to be on my side. Even though I had already confirmed with him that I knew that it wasn't a real marriage certificate. But that didn't matter to him. What they said didn't matter it's what he thought, what he wanted me to say. I told him that I can't do this anymore, there's no way I can get that money he wants, so he might as well forget about it. He said, but you can move mountains, you can do anything because of who you are. You have a way of getting that money, you can do it, do it for me, do it for our love, so we can be happy together.

At this point I couldn't see any way to do anything that would convince him that. He was warped in the head basically. I was disgusted with him at this point. He did not in any way shape or form prove anything to me or do anything for me really. I did all the work, I sacrificed everything, he didn't have to sacrifice anything even money. And he said to me that he was going to pay me every cent back. That he wanted me to have to trust me. Still trying to keep me in in his grasp. I said to him how can everyone else be lying, what is their purpose? They've got nothing to gain from lying to me. Why would they lie? He said, their terrorists…. (he was definitely odd, to him everyone was a terrorist) they're out to destroy our love. They don't want us to be together, they're trying to keep you from me. They want to keep me here that I can't leave. He even got to the point where he said, well, do you want me to video time you so that I can prove to you I am who I am. He had said this a few times in the past and I said yes, but he wouldn't do it. So where do you go from here, I thought to myself what I tell him, how can I make him listen to reason, because he wasn't answering any of my questions.

He was just talking about true love, that God put us together and it was fate that brought us together. That I just needed to believe. But I couldn't believe anymore, I couldn't see the point of any of it because I just kept having to put money out, I risked a lot already and I wasn't about to risk anymore on a one-sided love affair, even if it had to kill me. He wanted me to go see bikers, try and get the money from them and you know what, it's as if I went, I would be a dead woman. It didn't seem to matter to him what I had to give away, all that mattered to him was for me to get more money for him. I called him a selfish, evil person, who only thought of himself and devalued everyone else around him. And I said I was done, that I couldn't do this anymore. So, then he started yelling at me, saying Sue you are an evil witch, you're an Internet prostitute, you will die alone and feel pain. And many other things which I really don't want to express now. I guess but basically, I ended up at that point blocking him once again.

Chapter Eleven

THE NEW BEGINNING

PART ONE

And then my daughter out in BC wanted me to come to her. She was very concerned about my emotional state and with everything that was happening. She knew that my son and daughter-in-law didn't want me to be there, that they tried kicking me out a couple of times already. That between them and my oldest daughter, that they had blocked all my funds, which made me so that I I was penniless for over a month. I had to survive on what I had on me. That it was all about them, that they were the ones that were the victims, and I wasn't a victim whatsoever. I was just part of the process what happened to them. Prior to leaving to go to BC, I ended up having to do a phone call interview with my doctor, who ended up having to decipher whether I was sane or insane. At that point I was still with The Good Doctor (communicating only for information) he ended up wanting to make sure that I could get access to my funds. Hoping to get whatever he could from me. He wanted more of my money obviously. And I told him I had no way of getting any money at all. Not even a dime if I wanted. So, I had an interview on the phone with the doctor and she asked me a series of questions, if I felt suicidal, I said no, she asked about the situation that was at hand. I said to her, well, to be honest I fell in love with the man deeply, I thought it was true love and he did say he was going to pay me back. Take care of me forever and I said I got pulled into his world big time. I said yes, he was abusive and pushed me and pushed me, but then again you know, I was used to that because of my husband. And because I said that statement, she understood 100% because she knew what my husband was like, how hard it was for me and under those circumstances. She said yes, I can see how you ended up getting hooked into this whole situation. I even said to her, you know what's funny if I would have given my family the money, they wouldn't have thought I was insane, they just would have been happy to get it away from me. But because I gave it to a stranger, they deemed me insane. That remark also hit her home, because when she when I said that to her, she said yeah, I can see your point. And I said in the meantime, I didn't ask for help, I never did but I said they didn't offer me any help either. They're trying to say they're the victims and they're forgetting all about me and what happened to me. In the process that happened to me, how it happened to me, and how everything unfolded. I said not only did I find out that this man wasn't my true love, but I also found out the colors of my family, that I do not have a family anymore. That I don't get treated the same way, that no matter what I do they're going to look at me differently, they're going to mark me whatever way they want to mark me, I guess. I don't judge people, I don't blame them for feeling bad or mad, but it does hurt, regardless because I've always done everything I possibly could for my family. I would go to the ends of the earth for them. I just feel sad that my family has devalued their mother to a point that she is lost inside herself.

But I accept my fate, I accept what's going to happen to me, I must because I live for today. Yesterday is gone you can't change it, can't alter it and there's no take backs. So, we must accept our past. And tomorrow quite honestly is not guaranteed. I apologize for that little spit in the middle there, I just needed to get that out and let you know how things can transpire and change against you only because people don't understand what one goes through.

So, I get on a plane, and I go to my daughters in British Columbia because she had back surgery and needed her mother, wanted her mother. But she had an alternate plan as well because, she wanted to make sure her mom was okay. She wanted to know my emotional state when I was capable of whether I'd be able to handle myself properly and conduct things in a normal complacent manner. And apparently, she missed me very much and wants me to be a part of her life regardless. If I don't live with them but that they know where I am. But I ended up staying with her, I was only supposed to be there for a couple weeks but the second day, I was there supposed to be taking care of her, I went spelunking and ended up breaking my wrist in four places. Not too bad for a 63-year-old woman who just broke her first bone. So anyways, I ended up at the hospital where they had to put me out and reset my hand. But because the severity of the injury I could not get on a plane until it got to a point where it had healed. Where the cabin pressure wouldn't cause damage to my wrist. I even went and saw the surgeon 3 to 4 weeks before I had to come back for my trip home, He said, well, we're going to have to re-break your arm and I said why? He said, well, you're off 10 degrees. I looked at him and said, listen my brains off 10 degrees between the two I'm normal now, and who knows, maybe it'll improve my penmanship. You see regardless of everything this Good Doctor did to me, I still had a sense of humor, I could still think for myself.

Chapter Twelve

ONE LAST TIME

And no, the story doesn't end there, because he did contact me again when I was in British Columbia. It wasn't till about 2 ½ months after I was in BC that he ended up contacting me.

This is what happened.

Somehow, he ended getting back on my Hangouts profile. This is how the text went:

The Good Doctor: hey baby! Its been pretty long, I won't lie, I miss you a lot, I just can't wait to meet you someday in reality baby

Me: how is my favorite pen pal?

(Sends me happy face emoji.)

The Good Doctor: I knew you missed me a lot too, I Can feel from where I am, we are connected.

Me: so, how's life for you? I'm having so much fun, many things change, smile. Going to publish two books I am writing, talked to three publishers and now my life is opening for me. I don't need my family to do it, smile. How is your life? I feel free, alive, wonderful, had four marriage proposals and counting but unable to get my soul and body yet. Men are going out of their way just to be near me., being reborn has changed me so much. I am adventures awaiting, I've done many things, I wouldn't have done see places I wouldn't have seen.

The Good Doctor: Wow this is amazing.

Me: May my family kept me back and now I am just living my dream.

The Good Doctor: I am glad you are doing great, my wife is fine, remember we are still married.

Me: More than great am fantastic.

The Good Doctor: I love your tattoo baby.

Me: it's just a piece of paper, like money, thank you took 5 ½ hours to get to get it.

The Good Doctor: Yes babe, but because of this piece of paper, you left me to die in this war zone.

Me: This is boring, you know that right, why can't you just live life for today.,

The Good Doctor? What is boring?

Me: tomorrows not guaranteed.

The Good Doctor: you left me here to die, it's bad of you, me you left here to die.

Me: You left me high and dry in debt, which has gone from 80,000 to 20,000, smile, I'm doing just fine and getting better every day

NOTE: I KNOW I'M SOUNDING BUBBLY AND HAPPY, BUT I DIDN'T WANT TO GIVE HIM THE SATISFACTION OF HOW MUCH HE HURT ME. I WANTED HIM TO KNOW I AM ALIVE AND ABLE TO MOVE ON.

The Good Doctor: I did not leave you in debt, I have told you every penny spent to save me you will get back in double fold baby.

Me: That paper is no good anyway, because… we never consummated the marriage.

The Good Doctor: I know you have this money to save me, why are you holding back? Our marriage certificate is not just a paper, watch your words, you prefer drawing tattoos rather than save me.

Me: From the deadly war zone, right? You have you are being heartless towards me. I haven't wronged you in any way

Me: All I did was give you all my money, and that put me in debt, a lot of debt. YOU say that you will come to me, you know you can, but you won't. So, I am living in the now smile

The Good Doctor: I hate the fact that you don't trust your husband, but outsiders, you are so F##### annoying, Susan

Me: You funny, here we go again.

The Good Doctor: I am irreplaceable!!!!!!

Me: Maybe but you are not here, and I am not there. So, what can you do about it? I gave you what I have back then, what I want, I make what money I need for me, smile. Had it once and I will have it again. Smile, and much more, may only be a paper, but I found out you need it to live. God showed me what I needed to know, you haven't proven one thing to me in all our conversations, you... just a pen pal

The Good Doctor: baby I want to be with you my love, I have proposition for you baby.

Me: someone who is all talk, I know that your words are your only proof

The Good Doctor: it's risky for me because I do it against the rules of the base,

Me: lol... yeah... right it is I've heard this from your countless times.

The Good Doctor: I will talk to my technician, to arrange a shot video call, so you can see me, then you will have to believe I am real, but you will have to promise not to make any sounds, because the server here is encrypted to the Pentagon... that detects sounds and anyone flaunting the rules, at the base, I might lose my life if I am caught, but I have to do this, do it for love but it is with a price, you will have to promise to save me from the war zone? I am sincerely dying here baby, I am suffering baby, you need to save your husband hubby?? Doubting Thomas, you are there with me? You know I hate silence??

Me: do you really?

The Good Doctor: what is wrong with you Sue?

Me: It's me, I'm alive, baby, I am free, and I am a child of God and I have been reborn, I no longer fear life or people.

The Good Doctor: if you are truly a child of God, you won't allow me to die in this disaster of a place you are saying a different thing entirely babe.

Me: if you truly were a man, you say you are, you would do what you can to show me your love, words are just the shadow of a man

The Good Doctor: I want you to save me from here, what the hell is wrong with you? I propose something to you, but it seems you can't read any longer Susan

Me: seeing the real you are what I wanted from you, but you say you're going to and then don't

The Good Doctor: I will talk to the technician and arrange a video shot call so you can see me. Then you will have to believe I am real, but you will have to promise not to make any sound because the server here is encrypted to the Pentagon that dedicates sound and anyone flaunting the rules at the base, I might lose my life if I am caught but I have to do this for love but this is the price I have to pay to promise to save me from this war zone? Read through the lines carefully woman.

Me: If you are real and I mean real you know I would do anything to save you, but that comes at a price from you, I did your silly man.

The Good Doctor: what price woman?

Me: But I need to find a quiet place, where I am not where I am is not quiet, proof to me that you are who you are and for real.

The Good Doctor: I will arrange that for the video call, with you I will talk to the technician

Me: Sounds like a plan smile.

The Good Doctor: I am scared, but God will see me through it Amen.

Me: Amen

The Good Doctor: I am in a military base with much security and restrictions, which you are very much aware of baby.

Me: With the grace of God anything is possible, but you have to believe 100% only by your words

The Good Doctor: I believe, I want to see your beautiful face baby.

Me: When you find out let me know so I can have complete silence at my end, we'll have to arrange it that way because noisy here when they are all home/

The Good Doctor: okay baby, I love you baby, I miss you so much baby, I can't wait to be with you in reality baby, are we good now? Deep down in my heart I miss you a lot baby

Me: sorry I was on the phone with Dominic's girlfriend wanted to know if I could give him a ride.

The Good Doctor: okay babe did you miss me be sincere no lies

Me: you've been in all my thoughts, yes.

The Good Doctor: smile, you are mine forever.

Me: a part of me can never forget you.

The Good Doctor: it's been hell without you in my life baby, it was, I was surprised when I got your text from you today.

Me: hey, why, I'm the woman no man can own

The Good Doctor: I thought you have moved on with your life

Me: I have smile,

The Good Doctor: I accepted my fate to die here saving lives baby.

Me: I'm getting stronger and better.

The Good Doctor: I know my wife, she is strong like her husband, we were created for each other for life. I pray after calling you have a change of mind and save me from the deadly place.

Me: I'm confident and competent smile, I too simply, that's who I am

The Good Doctor: I trust you with everything in my, in me, I have faith in us.

Me: my phone is going to die sorry; I need to charge it.

The Good Doctor: OK.

Me: it only lasts maybe an hour after my flight back home, I look at getting a new phone.

The Good Doctor: I will get you a new phone, a better phone, when I come to you in in reality, it won't be long flight to were?

Me: Ontario smile

The Good Doctor: When is your flight?

Me: but not for long I not going to stay there but need to put closure for those that are.

The Good Doctor: okay baby, do you still love me? Are you still there my love?

And then without expecting it, it was like 10:30 at night in British Columbia. I was lying in my bed and my phone rang, it was a video chat. One I wasn't expecting whatsoever, and it was The Good Doctor. I was kind of stunned honestly, because I kept bugging him ever since I first met him that I wanted to see the real person. He looked just like his picture that he showed me. And it did take my heart. He was trying to pull up my heart and doing a good job of it too. But the first time he video chatted me it was only for about a minute, if that. But then he ended up video chatting me a second time, and he went over to the side of the bed, cocked his shoulders up, took a deep breath and jumped on the bed and just stared at me, not a word was said between us, but my lips moved, and I said, Why?

The Good Doctor: are you okay now?

Me: not sure.

The Good Doctor: I guess now you know I am real; I am mad at you for doubting my identity. I took the risk for you, and you are saying not sure? Didn't you see me?

Me: yes.

The Good Doctor: you look pretty baby I wish I was lying down with you over there.

Me: I don't know what to say.

The Good Doctor: You should know baby, my colleague just got inside the apartment. I am glad he never saw me on call with you, that was risky baby, you should learn to trust your husband baby. I am alive and real, I trust you, you look beautiful baby.

Me You don't know what this is doing to me.

The Good Doctor: What is happening to you baby? I have proven you wrong by showing you that I am real, went against the rules of the base to see your pretty face and also to show you my mind baby. You need to bring me home baby

Another Video chat from The Good Doctor and he just lies on the bed looking at me and I'm looking at him:

Me: I went through months of scrutiny. I have blocks on everything that has to do with money, family is difficult to say the least, there are many factors to all this. Like you really don't know, I am not sure I can ever put what has been going on to tell you.

The Good Doctor: Baby I know you have gone through a lot, even me too, my case is worse baby, I'm in a war zone.

Me: I wanted to just disappear but needed a passport so my family couldn't find me. I was going to run and hide, change my name, my identity, everything make myself disappear. I wasn't lying about offers from guys either, I find most men repulsive and pigs to say the least.

The Good Doctor: I know you love only me, so do I baby.

Me: They want one thing, which I really don't want. I know I have four men that want me forever all because I opened my mouth and say hello and smile.

The Good Doctor: smile, but they can't have you because you are my wife baby, you don't need to doubt me anymore, any longer, it hurts me a lot because I am going through a lot over here, I love you, Sue.

Me: Everything I did in the past was because I loved you, this is killing me here.

The Good Doctor: I love you baby, I have shown you that I am real baby, it's left to you to decide baby, my honored, my words baby.

Me: As soon as I wouldn't play the game, you called me terrible things, which I could never be.

The Good Doctor: I was almost caught, but the God of love saved me baby.

Me: The cop said the certificate was fake.

The Good Doctor: I was angry when you left me here to die baby. The cops will always say that trash to you, just to take away our happiness

Me: They said you're a con, a fake.

The Good Doctor: No one loves you better than I do baby, I will never hurt you, those are all lies baby.

Me And the girl denied working for the United Nations.

The Good Doctor: My love, this is the UN, we are talking about, dealing with terrorists, the girl is a UN agent which I haven't met before, but the UN knows her better. I am in a war zone, you know I have contact with anyone but you baby. Everyone is security conscious baby, you don't have to endanger my life baby

Me: look I can't hide who I am I am a humanitarian myself. I have people all the time my heart goes out too, you know that about me. I'm a good woman who cares for many people.

The Good Doctor: I am coming to you baby, I need you to know this, don't trust the cops they are dirty people, you know this already baby. I love you baby.

Me: Why hide from them? I don't understand that you can't lump them all under one an umbrella.

The Good Doctor: God will bear me witness that I have shown you that I am real against all odds baby, save me from this war zone or you will doubt me? When we're together, an hour would feel like a minute but when we are apart, a minute feels like an hour! I love you baby Sue.

Me: You know my thinking process; I need some time because you have my emotions at a peak here. I can't just switch off any everything else, this is very traumatic for me right now.

The Good Doctor: I've done my part; I pray you stop believing the rubber ship cops are telling you baby. We both love each other; you know this too well or do you have someone else? I will just have to kill myself then.

Me: Almost like shell shock.

The Good Doctor: Before this terrorist get to me, are we good now baby?

Me: please don't push me right now.

The Good Doctor: What is my position in your life now that you know I am real baby.??

Me: It's complicated.

The Good Doctor: I need to know; I'd being kept in the dark for too long, I am suffering baby. What is making complicated baby?

Me: I'm suffering too, That's why.

The Good Doctor: I can't wait for death to come take me from the terrorist I can't afford to lose my only woman I love, after I lost my late wife baby, nothing is complicated about us, you want to learn to follow your heart and not the people opinion baby

Me: Just like you had protocols, I need to process all my thoughts, it's not as easy as you think it would be, it's not black and white, it's not what you think it would be. I can't switch my thoughts like a light switch I'm sorry.

The Good Doctor: Honey, this is your sexy skyscraper husband you are talking about, baby. You can't just forget about me like that because the cops told you some untrue things about me. I work with the United Nations, and a military troop. I am here on a special assignment mission, it's confidential, if not it can endanger my life, and I would be killed by the wicked terrorists.

Me: Not sure what your end game is really, but I going to live a happy life, one way or another, and this queen is going to play the best game of chess. However, for the sake of love, because everything I did for you was out of love, and you just keep pushing. I don't know why money is important to you, never has been to me, but I will carry out my life as a tool, that old drunken ***** ....as you said, but yeah you had you put, you knew then you could go on to your next woman, of mad passion desire. That's what you wanted all along. I did say, I not the normal thinking woman, do I trust you, no, that is evident, but I need just over a month to figure out, how to get money to you. Every WAY or path I have is blocked on my end.

NOTE: I was pretending that I did have the money, to pay for his thing, because I wanted to see how he was going to react, and it was quite interesting. I just wanted you to see how he did things.

The Good Doctor: You are funny, you need a month to save me now, when you have left here several months to die. I have proven to you beyond reasonable doubt that I am for real. I can remember we are supposed to be together by now. But you left me here to die, claiming you have no money, not knowing you were busy listening to someone else. I guess, I asked you to help me. I wait here for long period now. I know you don't love me, and you don't want us to be together. I will die here saving lives, it's obvious you don't want to be with me Susan. For your information Susan, it's only money that can bring me to you. Mama it's all process, we have started, and we are almost done. Already. What happened to you, gave up on us, you became a chronic liar, an evil person, and also gave well for third party in our marriage. You are my wicked Susan, endangering my life, I know you want me dead

Me: Like I said you, you will get the money, I will get the money to save you, but I it comes to this. The queen needs to be better than anyone that could save her king from defeat, and you know, I told you the truth about everything. You know I did. You say everything bad about me, but down inside you know I am a damn good woman, who loves unconditionally, who would be willing at for sacrifice in the sake of love. You will be freed from there, and that was all you wanted it at the first place. Open But you will be freed, you don't need to talk to me anymore. I will let you know when I have a way to do it. You will have to wait till you here from me.

The Good Doctor: Who are you waiting for her, to get there before you save me?

Me: The person that's giving me the money to save you before the end of this month be flying here.

The Good Doctor: You are forgetting that I am in a war zone, it's dangerous out here.

Me: Life's gamble sweetheart, see I never get mad, smile, I may get go silent, but I don't say mean things for the most part. And you are a hypocritical man, you say you would never hurt me, never lie to me, yet I know from your true thoughts; I know that now it was in the being to get someone to save you. Was your ulterior motive, what happened I don't know, what wouldn't talked to me about your feelings, but you consistently got agree when I stopped sending money. You said you promised you would never hurt me, but yet you keep doing it.

The Good Doctor: You don't trust me, and I hate it. After all, what I went through to call you ….just to prove to you and your cop friends wrong, but, you still don't want to accept and believe in what we shared.

Me: the guy who has been helping me I do love you but that has nothing to do with trust because true love accepts you are you regardless of what you say or do or even act

The Good Doctor: Susan, you allow me to die in a war zone, and you expect me to be laughing with you? You allowed someone else to decide for you, in your, in our marriage, you don't listen to me but the cop guy, only I know what you have been doing all this while. We were connected, you already forget that fact. True love doesn't listen to the cop and doesn't investigate his or her partner.

I never did all these to you, but just gave you, my heart. But you keep betraying and deceiving me. I never knew you this way, my woman was better and sweeter than this version of you. Susan you are not being truthful with me, I can feel it. Who changed my wife?

Me: You look great, vibrant, pause… I loved everything. That is why I did what I did, and every time I say something now… you don't like it either, because even though my questions are valid, and logical you think you're an outright ghost, a skilled spoof, top secret undercover agent, that has his wife, who…is not even supposed to know you, know me for me, or you don't. I only lied when you told me because you of you, I learn to be a stronger person.

The Good Doctor: How did your daughter know you were still on Hangouts?

Me: Because she heard me crying in my room, and came, and read what you were saying to me.

The Good Doctor: I need to know I am being kept in the dark for too long, I am suffering baby. What is making it so complicated baby?

Me: I'm suffering too.

The Good Doctor: I can't wait for death to come take me from this earth. I can't afford to lose the only woman I love after I lost my wife, baby nothing is complicated about us, we ought to learn to follow our heart, and not people opinion baby

Me: Just like you have protocols, I need to process all my thoughts, it's not as easy as you think it would be. It's not black and white it's not what you think it would be I can't just switch my thoughts like a light switch I'm sorry

The Good Doctor: Why were you crying?

Me: Because of you because of the part of me that still believes in you.

The Good Doctor: Why would you cry because you saw me on a video call? You don't believe me.

Me: Because you were who I saw, the whole time we were a pen pal couple.

The Good Doctor: Mystery pointed me to the cop lover when did you become chronic liar?

NOTE: This was quite interesting, because every time I tried to let the cops know that he was in contact with me, or what he was saying, it may only take him five minutes to figure it out. By that time, I ended up going to the police station crossed the road from my daughter's place was. And yet he's still knew that the police he knew right away, and would text me saying, how dare you go to the police ABOUT ME. I spoke with him. How did he know? I would really like to know.

Me: That too was on the scrutiny of my daughter LOL, you don't stop.

The Good Doctor: There is no atom of truth in all you just said Susan.

Me: I cried most of last night, I was glad you were safe and so handsome and spry, the way you jumped on that bed

The Good Doctor: I gave you my heart.

Me: And I'm being 100% honest with you, can't believe what you want I can't help what you think and I know the truth one thing is I ******* still love you even though you stabbed me

The Good Doctor: I did not stab you, instead you did.

Me: I'm sorry but you screwed me.

The Good Doctor: I have called you and proven that I am real, I saw your pretty face too.

Me: You always get defensive and paranoid. I can't help your thoughts. How do you know so much about what I doing and who I with?

The Good Doctor: But you don't seem to believe me, we are connected, God shows me everything you do, I dream of you and see you and see it.

Me: Belief is a perception, it's what you see, I know what it feels like and reconnected with that, that is one of the ******* reasons when I saw you, I was shocked.

The Good Doctor: I have told you what we share is divine.

Me: I don't know if you saw my lips move, I said why?

The Good Doctor: I did, saw you properly, I am glad you are still pretty and gorgeous as always.

Me: look I only had my husband, even when I was sheltered from other people, I was I, because I care too much for the safety and care of people. I have always done that, you knew that.

The Good Doctor: I am not safe where I am, you are not saying anything concerning saving my life.

Me: Anything you ask me, I would say the same thing, even 10 years download line, but there can only be one true answer. That way you remember when it is repeated you say the same thing, the truth. How can telling the truth be lying? I didn't tell you this, but, three weeks ago God came to me. Because of how I was feeling and touched my soul again one night. I asked God to send me my true love and then you text me, now as a woman who believes in something with her whole heart take this. I was shocked, emotional, and very vulnerable. I am sorry, but when something you want comes into one's life, how does one comprehend that. I can't change what I feel or how I live, but I do believe me. I can do it and change my path. I can do it I know it because I have done it.

The Good Doctor: What do you mean baby, I am lost here, you can do what,

Me: I can walk away from anything and start over. I know I've done it and became a better version of myself. I don't hold grudges and I'm not by spot.

The Good Doctor: I don't hold grudges either.

Me: I accept and move on.

The Good Doctor: God kept me alive all this while, in this war zone, you are still saving me or not?

Me: I will but like I said, you must wait, just takes time, but you will be free and then you can let go of me smile.

The Good Doctor: Remember we are married for better or worse, we are supposed to be with each other forever, but you abandoned me to die in the wicked place. I can't let you go. I cannot let go of my wife; I am married to you.

Me: Oh, my young grasshopper one does not know what one as, Doth thou protest, it is in God's way to forgive yourself. For your fellow man. Over the past few months my belief my soul and my heart has been for God, He has shown me my path that I need to be on. Yes, for you it's my time to shine and give your life, to be free you, have ye little faith.

NOTE: I did this because he was always using God s a way to get to me.

The Good Doctor: Are you kidding me?

Me: One does what one needs to do, for you and within the month you will be freed, and I will be married smile.

The Good Doctor: amount.

Me: You will get your money before I would smile.

The Good Doctor: Wed who?

Me: So there you go, if you want your money, ask my son in law he's loaded, here's one of his cars and I sent him a picture of a Corvette with me smiling in front of it which does belong to my son in law by the way.

The Good Doctor: What is wrong with you, your hand? And why are you referring to me to your son.

Me: if I did a typo, whoops not my son in law.

The Good Doctor: I guess someone bought a new ride for herself and left me here to die it's unfair.

Me: Not mine, my son in laws he's loaded you may have been out if you didn't keep stopping me from coming here back then, but you wanted me where you where I was just grinding my gears out of love, and respect I listen to you. Right now, we both know things aren't going to get resolved today

The Good Doctor: When I say it's going to be, OK? You have kept me in the dark for too long. I don't deserve such treatment from you Susan.

Me: Know something sometimes one must see the darkness before they can see the light God's words.

The Good Doctor: Smile, I miss you so much.

Me: Need to say goodnight, so you know, that way she doesn't bug me again.

The Good Doctor: Are we back together? I need to know my place in your life right now.

Me: I don't know, my love for you is very strong, but maybe it's too strong right now, I'm torn.

The Good Doctor: Smile, but why are you still doubting my person and also reporting me to your cop lover friend Susan? I trust you with my life, why are you hurting me? I broke protocol for you.

Me: Doesn't know wife have the right to know the true identity of her husband????

The Good Doctor: To prove how much I want to be with you in reality baby. I called you to prove you wrong, but you still reported me, why, would you do that? There is no love without trust no lies.

Me: My daughter made me do that the next morning. This I can prove you wrong, did you read my poem, what about trust I said I say more about such a double barrel word as that.

The Good Doctor: I hate it when the one person I love, cherish, and call my only family, distraught distressed me, I am human, I have feelings. I get hurt a lot, where am I living at is a war zone, and I am going through a lot of difficult times here, my fight for survival is being God. We have proven to you beyond reasonable doubt that I am real, and alive, but you must save me.

Me: God is my God through, am I feel find peace, compassion, and love. In serenity of life really helps to be reborn twice smile, but one must be honest to achieve this. That I can say because God guides me obscure as that is, it true.

The Good Doctor: So, what is God telling you concerning saving your husband from the war zone? Before I die here.

Me: the plan is for me to save you but sacrificing me okay I made the deal

The Good Doctor: You made a deal with who?

Me: Then I can be all those things you claim me to be.

Me: Come on you know that a fake certificate right.

The Good Doctor: My love, you must tell God that now is the time to save me, if you truly love me. I don't know, he should help you ASAP.

The Good Doctor: Well, back to this certificate again.

Me: LOL.

The Good Doctor: You and your cop lover.

The Good Doctor sends me several happy face emojis.

Me: No, I can wed, someone else, why because you know it's not real that bothers you. Doesn't it that. That's why you keep asking if I found someone else.

The Good Doctor: What we share is divine, you can't leave me, we are glued together for life babe.

The Good Doctor: I laugh at you; no man can take you from me.

Me: Well then to save you, I guess I have to I go to jail then, one time.

The Good Doctor: Our certificate is legal, you can't choose to believe whatever you wish, but I pray you find this money, you will see me with you someday, that will prove everyone wrong.

The Good Doctor: I am real, you have seen me.

The Good Doctor: I am fine with that.

The Good Doctor: I have no point to prove to anyone else again, I am not well in this war zone.

The Good Doctor: Save me my beloved wife!

Me: And you look very healthy too. I need to get some sleep, it's 9:40 here and the time change. I need to clear my head, reset, was up most of last night.

The Good Doctor: okay babe.

The Good Doctor: I kiss you goodnight my beloved wife, I believe you will have a change of heart and save me from this disaster of a place.

The Good Doctor: You look beautiful on that on the call baby.

The Good Doctor: Doesn't let me get over you.

The Good Doctor: sends me an emoji hug twice.

The Good Doctor: hi.

Me: hello

The Good Doctor: We finally came here.

Me: Sorry went on a walkabout, they fun.

The Good Doctor: OK, what is your time zone now?

Me: It helps clear my mind and soul it's 8:53, I was debating on which mountain I want to climb, smile.

The Good Doctor: Mount Everest.

The Good Doctor: it's still early with you over there.

Me: Maybe Mount Baldy, yes, it is.

The Good Doctor: How are you doing today?

Me: I'm fantastic.

The Good Doctor: How about your night, did you dream about us?

Me: I didn't sleep as much as I thought I would, was up at 4.

The Good Doctor: What happened?

Me: My hand was hurting.

The Good Doctor: I am so sorry; I wish I was there with you help ease the pain pirate. I would have given you a soft massage, I guess you don't want me anymore in your life

Me: you are my favorite pen pal.

The Good Doctor: Smile, how many pen pals do you have now?

The Good Doctor: You call me the favorite, are you implying that I am no longer your sexy skyscraper has been in again?

Me: Time maybe, but right now I need to focus on getting things done. My time short here, I am going back for closure for the kids. Then who knows where I will be living. I can pick where I want to be and to choose who I want to be with, smile. You did make me realize that I needed someone for me and me alone, smile. I'm grateful for that, but in a month because God when he came in my dream three weeks ago, he said, I would soon be living my dream life. That I have seen the darkness and despair and shone a light of happiness for me. He saw how I was taunted and being tortured. Torturing myself, he knew I was and it was time for me to blossom like a rose.

The Good Doctor: I don't understand all what you are saying.

Me: okay LOL I wrote this poem and I want you to hear it,

If I were a rose
just as the sun begins to rise,
I look up with my big brown eyes
I see the seed of life it grows
In the sand as the water flows
As days go by its leaves appear
Our bud upon the stem comes near
It starts to radiate a color to be
That blossoms red for all to see
For just like me I watch it pose
Oh yes, my love it is just a rose

The Good Doctor: Your way is not straight, be forward any longer.
Go I won't force myself on you

Me: Yes, and you will be free, that was your main objective and
that will happen I will see to it.

The Good Doctor: You have bluntly refused to say anything about
saving me any longer. I guess you don't care about humans lives
again, if I die here, my blood is on you.

The Good Doctor: Why are you refusing to meet me again in
reality?

The Good Doctor: I am your husband for crying out loud.

The Good Doctor: I am not doing well where I am, you need to
save me woman.

The Good Doctor: You talk a lot of irrelevant things this moment.

The Good Doctor: I am not interested in anything but meeting you in reality.

Me: You need to calm down now take a breath.

The Good Doctor: if you don't want to meet me in reality any longer, just let me if want out, I am tired of your devious lifestyle towards me.

Me: you put yourself there, I didn't.

The Good Doctor: You can't sit at the comfort of your home and tell me to calm down, when I am suffering over here

The Good Doctor: You are a wicked to humanity Susan.

The Good Doctor: How can someone be this heartless.

The Good Doctor: **** you are getting on my nerves Susan.

Me: I told you time it is what it is needed, except it refuse it. It up to you, I can't stop what you think or feel

The Good Doctor: Tell me what I want to hear and not this rubbish you are writing.

Me: if you're not happy with me then be honest with yourself, let go if you have to. I would understand, but I have a process too

The Good Doctor: Christmas is drawing closer, we need to be together, can't you see this woman?

Me: This is hard for me right now.

The Good Doctor: Nothing is hard for you stop lying.

Me: I do move mountains, smile.

The Good Doctor: You are not well.

Me: Smile. Think what you wish for you, better choose your words wisely because hurting or pushing the one person willing to help you, is a bad thing.

The Good Doctor: Woman, any amount of money you spent, have spent to save me you will get in double fold. I am not begging you to continue this process you lie a lot lately.

The Good Doctor: A ******* process you do have to wait this long to save me from this war zone Susan?

The Good Doctor: You are annoying Susan.

Me: Wow, I couldn't be more honest than I am right now to you, do not trust me and okay that is your choice sweetheart, but in reality, I am as true as the sun rises every morning.

The Good Doctor: You have left me here too for too long to die, while you are touring around the globe tattoo in your body.

Me: I just don't know if I love you now is all, but a part of me is fighting tha.t

The Good Doctor: meeting men like you always tell me.

Me: They meet me, I don't look for them

The Good Doctor: **** you and your suitor's woman, save me from the war zone, tell me something meaningful.

Me: But I don't go to bed with them either.

The Good Doctor: it's your business.

Me: And its short chats but you don't care about me, it's all about you getting out.

The Good Doctor: When are you making the complete payment?

Me: You never care about me.

The Good Doctor: I am very direct now.

Me: Smile, are you!!!!!

The Good Doctor: I don't have time for your lies.

The Good Doctor: A lot these days.

The Good Doctor: When are you making the complete payment?

Me: On the 3rd of December is the earliest I can do anything. I must be there to do it, and you don't have to talk to me until then. I have things ready for you I will praise a prize you closer to the date as so that you get your money, and you can be happy doing whatever you want to do that was your end of the game anyway.

The Good Doctor: What game?

The Good Doctor: Why can't you make payment this week?

NOTE: Now I am really playing with his mind, just so you know and possibly by reading what I wrote, I was going in circles with them only because I wanted to hurt this ******* because he hurt me so bad.

Me: Getting what you want, me as your puppet. I understand what and why you did this, and I Was never the end game, I have to be in Ontario.

The Good Doctor: Troublesome Ontario.

Me: It's where the money is plans to be able to do by Bitcoin, so it be untraceable for you. Need to charge my phone, but will let you know when you when, so you would be rid of the evil lying queen.

The Good Doctor: Honey, you will have long for a better Bitcoin machine that accepts a better amount of money.

Me: You don't have to pretend to love me to get it OK, they do up to 100,000 there.

The Good Doctor: I love you that why I am still here.

The Good Doctor: where?

Me: Ontario.

The Good Doctor: You can make a payment up to worth 10,000 euros in some machines, I want to come to you baby sorry €10,000.

Me: I know and you will get it, I can't do it here and I have to be there to do it, there is one in Barrie that does 100,000.

The Good Doctor: Where you are you now?

Me: Just plug my phone in and going to make a tea.

The Good Doctor: Do you mean 10,000 or 100,000?

Me: 100,000 just like I wrote.

The Good Doctor: You and your tea as usual

Me: Yes always, it calms me.

The Good Doctor: interesting.

The Good Doctor: I know you love your tea.

The Good Doctor: Where are you now?

The Good Doctor: The city?

Me: on my bed

The Good Doctor: Smile good.

The Good Doctor: Bad girl.

Me: Not a city, a town.

The Good Doctor: okay what is the name of the town?

Me: Oliver.

The Good Doctor: There should be a BITCOIN machine there baby, we have been to silent for long time, the banister and the UN need to hear from us baby.

The Good Doctor: it would be bad the entire process is truncated on the UN due to our silence baby?

The Good Doctor:??

Me: Sorry I need to let my phone charge, then email them if you must.

The Good Doctor: You have to email them baby, I am scared of dying here. I want to rest in your arms baby.

The Good Doctor: I am suffering over here; I pray you don't find yourself in a war zone.

The Good Doctor: You will understand better.

Me: Right, what you want to send to me OK.

Me: I wanted to talk to Sean, behalf hour or so.

The Good Doctor: I want you to do it with your heart, while it hurt, write it. Also includes my email address

The Good Doctor: Tell them you want to continue the process, that I want should be pardoned that it was due to some unseen circumstances, that caused the delay.

The Good Doctor: okay babe, do take care of yourself. With an emoji kiss

The Good Doctor: You didn't say anything.

Me: Sorry, walking.

The Good Doctor: Read my last text and give me an answer?

Me: Am so ******* confused right now

The Good Doctor: You shouldn't be baby.

The Good Doctor: I know my wife; she is too smart to be confused.

Me: Well, she's freaking out.

The Good Doctor: impossible.

The Good Doctor: I need an answer now baby soon.

Me: I'd be fine OK,

The Good Doctor: I don't get you?

Me: I will handle it OK.

The Good Doctor: Win baby? Me today.

The Good Doctor: okay my love.

The Good Doctor: I will send you places where you can find Bitcoin machines at all over.

The Good Doctor: What do you think?

Me: They don't have any and my phone going to die and money in Ontario.

The Good Doctor: Do you think so Princess?

Me: I know so.

So, then The Good Doctor decides to send me three different locations in BC with complete address, etc. As to where some bitcoin machines would be located for me to go and send him the money. I didn't disclose This information because of the legal factors. I couldn't say. That he could pull up that information here in Ontario or Canada or wherever. Because he always seemed to be able to do that whenever he wanted me to use a bitcoin machine, just so that I'd know a location of where it would be. When I asked him, he said, well we're trained to know how to read maps etc. But that means he would have had to download locations to find out where you could do bitcoin machines. He would have to use the Internet, (so doesn't that kind of compromise his location if they're trying to keep it secret?!) To me that always seemed odd, but when I asked him, as he said was well, we're trained to knowing how to use maps. Would never elaborate any further on that.

The Good Doctor: Honey check the addresses out; I have three for you.

The Good Doctor: Where are you?

Me: LOL, I don't have a car to get there, and closes is 2 hours by car and the cash is in Ontario.

The Good Doctor: How much do you have in Ontario baby?

The Good Doctor: I want to spend Christmas with you baby, the fast-approaching baby.

Me: Funny it's the last thing I'm thinking of I should have all what you need one shot.

Me: Christmas, I mean I would go to church.

NOTE: Now, I started playing the game a bit more with him, and I ended up writing a letter to the United Nations and this is what I wrote. And then sent to him. I had no money, nothing, I went consumer proposal; ok. I wanted him to know what wanting something and them finding out the pains are not getting what you want to feel like. I am I nice person, he was evil. He hurt me, I know I shouldn't have lied, but he lied to me since day one.

> Dear Sir, this is regarding The Good Doctor,
> who is currently serving in the UN humility

humanitarian position with the government. I have been unable to respond till now because of some unforeseen circumstances and am here to inform you that the money he owed in taxes should be finalized by the first week of December. Thank you in advance for your patience. Susannah.

Then I sent him the copy. I did it but I was using AI to do it because I didn't have the money anyway. I Knew it all was fake anyway at that point, there was no way he could convince me that it wasn't.

The Good Doctor: okay my love.

The Good Doctor: You are always intelligent.

The Good Doctor: indeed, you are my wife, I am always proud of you baby.

The Good Doctor: We would be going to church together on Christmas Day.

The Good Doctor: Where are you now?

Me: Well, I would believe it when I see it, that all I can say.

The Good Doctor: Smile, I will be with you baby, I will make it alive from this war zone.

Me: Until then my thoughts are unclear as to what going to happen.

The Good Doctor: God will keep me safe for you.

The Good Doctor: What is going to happen my love?

The Good Doctor: Share your thoughts with me baby.

Me: I don't know yet because I haven't made up my mind.

The Good Doctor: Concerning us?

Me: But I know I am a woman of my word, I feel your just saying things to get what you want truthfully your trying to get out of a bad spot

The Good Doctor: Honey you are my wife, you are my only family.

Me: You have a son.

The Good Doctor: I am dying silent over here baby.

The Good Doctor: You need to save your husband before I am gone forever from the surface of the earth.

Me: What happened was all my children doing not mine.

The Good Doctor: I trust and believe in you only.

Me: Thanks, but I know you don't, not till you see the money.

The Good Doctor: Are you telling me the truth baby?

Me: That what I think yes because your words are quite specific

The Good Doctor: Baby, I want to be with you in reality, to prove all does doubting my existence wrong.

The Good Doctor: I am alive baby.

The Good Doctor: I can't hurt or fly.

The Good Doctor: I left my life for people at my age, I deserve to rest, and be happy before death takes me out of the surface of this earth.

The Good Doctor: I hate the fact that you doubted my existence too.

Me: Not your existence, your intention.

The Good Doctor: I would never treat you that way, knowing you are in a war zone.

Me: I have nothing to offer you

The Good Doctor: My intentions are harmless baby.

Me: Why me?

The Good Doctor: Can't you feel the true love?

The Good Doctor: Ask our creator that question babe.

Me: That the hard part for me, I do not know what true love is.

The Good Doctor: He is in a better position to give you the answer you seek babe.

The Good Doctor: Two of his, what we share now, I am coming to you in reality, to show you true love, treat you like a queen that you are.

Me: That why I'm confused, I asked him to show me my true love.

The Good Doctor: The truth is, we are connected and also created for each other, that is the reality no man can separate us, unless God says otherwise.

The Good Doctor: I am your true love; don't I give you happiness and rest of mind babe?

The Good Doctor: I am the best man for you.

The Good Doctor: You knew how we started baby.

The Good Doctor: Distance couldn't be a barrier in our love. (With an emoji heart)

The Good Doctor: You didn't answer this question, how much do you have in Ontario?

Me: I did it hidden safe.

The Good Doctor: I can still remind you how much we are still owing for my accumulated taxes babe.

Me: Only I know.

The Good Doctor: (emoji happy face)

The Good Doctor: How much in total babe?

Me: Almost $200,000. (This was a lie)

The Good Doctor: Yes baby.

The Good Doctor: I am glad God made it possible for you to have this funds to save me, finally ...so we can be together soon.

The Good Doctor: How long have you been saving this money for babe?

The Good Doctor: Indeed, you move mountain.

The Good Doctor: Are you still their baby?

Me: Sorry was on phone with a friend.

The Good Doctor: okay babe.

The Good Doctor: How long have you been saving this funds babe?

The Good Doctor: You haven't answered me yet baby.

Me: Since you were mean to me.

The Good Doctor: I am not mean to you; you were on to me couple months. (Notice his words, (You were on to me))

The Good Doctor: Are you working now baby?

Me: No, I'm off today, how did you know I was working, doing jobs?

The Good Doctor: We are connected babe.

The Good Doctor: God shows me a lot about us.

Me: I need to know something.

The Good Doctor: We are created for each other babe.

The Good Doctor: What do you need to know, again?

Me: What is it about me that you see in me?

The Good Doctor: I love you for no reason because if I have a reason for loving you, someday I will have one to leave babe.

The Good Doctor: My love for you is genuine and real you know it.

The Good Doctor: Just be you.

The Good Doctor: Stop living your life for anyone, your happiness should be your priority.

Me: That is what makes me, it's a part of me who I am.

The Good Doctor: At our age we need to be happy, and we also know what we want.

Me: That a true statement.

The Good Doctor: I can feel you smiling, right now.

Me: My phone is going to die again.

The Good Doctor: You feel more relaxed with me.

The Good Doctor: Where are you now baby?

Me: in the garage.

The Good Doctor: Where are you working now?

The Good Doctor: What are you doing in the garage babe?

Me: Have a couple of jobs bookkeeping, and supervisor at shoppers.

The Good Doctor: How much do they pay baby, monthly?

Me: Not all that great but enough make couple of 1000 doing books, and couple thousand at shoppers.

NOTE: I know that statement was a lie, I was just trying to play along with his game, just so you're aware of it. This, I know, was wrong to do, but this guy hurt me, this guy lied to me, I wanted to bring him down hard, I wanted him to believe I was on his side. Now reading what I did, doesn't make me proud of what I did. I was stooping to his level.

Me: Only one supervisor to contend with, my phone is going to die again chords are inside I'm outside.

The Good Doctor: Go and charge your phone babe. I have missed you so much.

The Good Doctor: hi babe!

Me: Forgot to plug in phone, or it died now on charge I need to go do somethings.

The Good Doctor: You are so busy lately, you hardly have time here babe.

The Good Doctor: Where are you now?

Me: As a matter of fact, yes, I plugged it in but wasn't plugged in the wall, was going to do something and you dinged me. LOL phone is where I sleep. I've been busy a lot lately, busy mind makes a calm soul.

The Good Doctor: You have been busy doing what?

The Good Doctor::??

Me: I used to imagine you as I saw you the other night, and because I truly believed you were my soulmate. I did want I did for you, and I came across this little gem a "life is a challenge, make it, life is sorrow, overcome it. Life is life fight for it.", these quotes came from a mother, from Mother Teresa, so then what am I to think the quote is empowering and deep to my soul.

The Good Doctor: My love, I have been busy saving lives, how are you?

At this point I sent him a picture of me and Sue doing a chat.

The Good Doctor: You look beautiful (emoji happy face)

Me: But I come to realize that I am not a me person, I am a person I care about people that's why I'm different than the norm. I care about others above myself, you know its never about money to me. I'm far from materialistic as one can be. I am the only one that can get the only thing I need to make my life right for me. Is to find someone who loves me for me accepts me for me I know you don't that's the hard truth

The Good Doctor: Honey, I accepted you the way you are restore your self-esteem back, made you my woman, I love you genuinely it pains me a lot when you doubt me, because I will never do that to you baby.

The Good Doctor: I have told you countless times, that we are connected baby.

The Good Doctor: We can't lie to ourselves baby.

The Good Doctor: We can't lie to ourselves baby.

The Good Doctor: We shouldn't let outside siders to decide for us in our marriage baby, I love you dearly and you know it.

The Good Doctor: All I desire is to be in your arms baby.

The Good Doctor: I want a peaceful life with you.

Me: Maybe we are, but I had to see the darkness before I could see the light. The truth, your preconceived thoughts of who I am is so wrong, it's backwards. I have lost all credibility with those I care about, the most. Because of the deceptions. And lies you made to me, made me do.

The Good Doctor: Stop saying all this baby, I am coming to you.

The Good Doctor: You did it for my safety baby.

The Good Doctor: I am coming to you to fix everything; you need to be positive baby.

Mel: look where it got me, but I'm better for it because I know my path now.

The Good Doctor: What is your path now baby?

The Good Doctor: Honey, I don't have all the words to express how much you mean to me. I can only say that you are the center of my life, and everything else revolves around our love for each other.

Me: I'm going to live, have fun and maybe even skin on skin. Whereas, whoever I want, because I feel I deserve to have fun be happy. Go wild maybe, I even become an alcoholic and take drugs and be the tramp you keep saying I am. Adventures awaits think like a me person, instead of a God child. I want to be happy, maybe living in a moment it was what I need, instead of thinking my body is only for one sole purpose

Me: How I feel about love, read this, if you want to know what in my heart.

I loved you from the very start your words were sweet, your wits were fun

You make me smile and glow like the morning sun

I cannot tell you that I want you TO GO

But my love for you is like a fresh fallen snow

There is only one thing that I really fear

As if I can't have you over here

I love you then I love you now

I just wonder when and how

The day I wish is so dear to me

That I want to be with you, you see

I only AM syncing with my heart

For you I just wish upon the day

I can't say I do

That was my wish

The doctor sent me a huge heart throbbing. Imago.

The Good Doctor: I love you, genuine baby, and I will be with you, in reality. I'm going through difficult times over here; I am supposed to be with my wife. But I know God's time is the best.

The doctor I will keep praying to stay alive for me to meet you someday in reality.

The Good Doctor: I know you will save me.

The Good Doctor: I trust your prowess, baby.

The Good Doctor: I know the woman I got married to. I can't wait to have your skin to skin with you my beautiful Princess.

Me: I'm tired of caring for others you know that everyone expects me to fix all their problems. I feel like being invisible and no one can find me just like you are

The Good Doctor: Baby we are connected, I understand you, but don't I give you happiness?

Me: I feel I need to be more selfish than to be selfless.

The Good Doctor: that's not you baby, be you baby, no one should make you change your person.

Me: That tattoo and my spontaneous approach to life should be my next move.

The Good Doctor: I love the tattoo baby, it's fine

The Good Doctor: I love you for no reason baby.

Suzana Thayer

The Good Doctor: I know you are annoying most times, but you are mine.

The Good Doctor: I can't do away with you.

The Good Doctor: We need to make this marriage work baby.

The Good Doctor: I am coming to you.

Me: I only had three hours sleep; I need to lie down sorry.

The Good Doctor: That's not my baby.

The Good Doctor: I always put you to bed.

The Good Doctor: You hardly leave me here.

The Good Doctor: You are acting weird baby.

The Good Doctor: I am not allowing you to go to bed now.

The Good Doctor: We haven't heard from each other for a long time.

Me: This is someone who found out how greedy people are, and how it easy to abandon family. A person and one that is the only one that would be there for others, regardless of her own needs or desires. He made me see that I needed someone in my life, someone that would accept all my flaws and loved me for me. I am really tired I feel sick to my stomach for real, not figuratively speaking

The Good Doctor: Sincerely you are not sounding well with me.

The Good Doctor: it seems you are in a bad mood

134

Me: WHAT DO YOU WANT FROM ME?

Me: You're driving me crazy.

The Good Doctor: I am your husband for crying out loud. I was supposed to be with you right now. You claim to forget what we share Susan?

The Good Doctor: You are fine, I am irreplaceable, you know that this this is reality baby

The Good Doctor:??

Me: I seem to know a lot yet nothing, and I never fought in my life with anyone till I met you, must be my passion are for doctors right, the best view I've had here was with surgeons.

The Good Doctor: I will fight to death for true love. It's rare to find baby.

Me: No one knows that better than me, but sometimes you can't get what you want, I've lived it for years and It's not going to break me. I won't let it.

The Good Doctor: What are you saying baby? Are you not bringing me to you any longer?

Me: Never said that, for being a smart man you are dumb.

The Good Doctor: I am so dumb?

The Good Doctor: Interesting, give me what I what you have?

Me: You can't imagine how you make me feel because you drive me nuts.

The Good Doctor: How do I drive you nuts?

Me: I only wanted to save you, what the hell is wrong with that.

The Good Doctor: Nothing is wrong with that.

Me: You seem to take my words out of context. I am who I am. I am a child of God, and I'm saying the Lord's name over and over, "I am that I am".

The Good Doctor: I am also a child of God too.

The Good Doctor: I am too.

The Good Doctor: I want to be with you in reality, I am going through a lot here.

The Good Doctor: I can't take it anymore; I deserve to be happy and live a peaceful life at my age.

The Good Doctor: I want you to speak the truth, when you are bringing me home?

The Good Doctor: Let's be sincere to ourselves baby.

Me: You read what I wrote to the barrister right?

The Good Doctor: Yes baby.

Me: Have I let you down when I said what I would be doing???

The Good Doctor: No baby

The Good Doctor: I trust you.

Me: You will be free and be able to do what you want; however you want OK.

The Good Doctor: But we have been apart for too long and you also don't trust me.

The Good Doctor: You are torturing me over here.

Me: Trust isn't a factor.

The good doctors: Smile.

Me: I'm saving you.

The Good Doctor: okay baby.

Me: What else do you want, I'm only one person.

The Good Doctor: Which Bitcoin machine accepts 100,000 baby?

Me: The one on Dunlop.

The Good Doctor: How do you know that?

Me I used it to send you money, tells us how much it will do.

The Good Doctor: I guess it should 10,000 euros are not 100,000.

The Good Doctor: Make the payment in little segments,15,000 euros I don't want anything screwed up. I want to be with you baby. I have been far too long baby

Me: Sorry I dozed off, I banged my bad hand and don't want anyone to know, because I need to get home. I don't want them to re break it again, it's not healed every time I go, they want to re break it. I'm not going back there, maybe I put it where it should be anyway, do not one of them to do it again.

The Good Doctor: Baby you are going through lots of pains please stop stressing your hand.

Me: I need to make it look like it's OK.

The Good Doctor: Did you read my previous message about the payment?

Me: Being hiding it so long, so no one knows yeah.

The Good Doctor: Baby, please take it easy, this is the major reason you need me around, to take care of it for you baby.

Me: I must I have become a good liar now, I want out of here, where I am. I don't want to go back there either, because of you, but I have no choice. Remember your words to get the money. I need to be there they won't let me go on a plane because of my wrist, I need to play this out.

The Good Doctor: How do you play with it, baby?

Me: By making it seem like my hands OK, just can't wear the brace on the plane, apparently, they said something about the cabin pressure.

The Good Doctor: Promised me baby.

Me: I don't get it I promise.

The Good Doctor: okay baby I love you always.

Me: God is my witness.

The Good Doctor: I am used to you, (with a great big, huge hug and a heart throbbing, emoji)

The Good Doctor: Honey, when I am in your presence, my heart is full, and I feel stronger, Wiser, and more confident. You inspire me to reach deep into my heart and love you with all of my passion I have.

Me: I'm shaking.

The Good Doctor: What is making you shake baby?

Me: My hand is cold, not eating... picked one or all the above, lack of sleep how the hell do I know.

The Good Doctor: Why are you refusing to sleep baby?

The Good Doctor: We overcame that.

The Good Doctor: What happened again?

Me: Pick one of the above.

The Good Doctor: I am here now.

The Good Doctor: It will be fine baby.

Me: I have enough drugs to kill a horse and yet me being a long a drug addict. I won't take them, I don't like taking them, yet they are the only thing I can take, because of how I react to other meds. I take my 12 hours at night that's it.

The Good Doctor: I understand everything baby, we have been through this before, God will see us through this baby.

The Good Doctor: Does it reduces the pain baby?

Me: A little bit, but some days nothing. I have a high pain threshold, but there are times it's beyond my control

The Good Doctor: I can't wait to be with you.

The Good Doctor: I feel my wife's pain already.

Me: Your getting ready for work.

The Good Doctor: You are going to work, or you eating, resting?

Me: resting

The Good Doctor: Good one.

Me: Well now my hands, rubbing, better than a stabbing pain, must have moved something. There's also a piece floating in there, that doesn't help but for my first break I did a did good job I broke it in four places, impressed.

The Good Doctor: You deserve rest, when you are up, you write me baby.

Me: I find it annoying really.

The Good Doctor: Your hand will fine again baby.

The Good Doctor: For real, I will fix everything when I come to you, I am handicap from this war zone. *

Me: I know, he told maybe because of the break could be take a year. I will text if I have time.

The Good Doctor: I know I will be with you in reality and take good care of you

The Good Doctor: I am always with you baby.

The Good Doctor: if you are game to sext, I am also.

The Good Doctor: You know we are connected baby.

The Good Doctor: I guess you are asleep already.

The Good Doctor: Hi baby.

The Good Doctor: write back when you are awake (two emoji kisses)

NOTE: About a week later.

The Good Doctor: Why the sudden silence from you?

The Good Doctor: What is wrong with you?

The Good Doctor: I hate the fact that you keep reading my texts and ignoring it, it hurts me so much that you are so heartless, what kind of a soul are you carrying?

The Good Doctor: You are becoming rude, and you won't like it, if become so to you?

The Good Doctor: I hate lies and deceit you should know me by now. I will always know what you are up to?

NOTE: A week after he wrote that I replied.

Me: You wouldn't accept the truth; you have destroyed my life. I had to claim bankruptcy because of you. I have no one to turn to because of you. I know now have no life thanks to you, but I still am in love with you, that alright… I don't understand.

The Good Doctor: true love really exists you can't deny that fact.

Me: It does, but it doesn't when it's only one-sided.

The Good Doctor: How is it one-sided.

Me: When one-sided is expected to do all the work, give till they bleed, until they are down, hurting and in pain. While the other doesn't believe them and keeps pushing for more without any remorse. Not caring about the one who tried so hard to save the person and didn't try to reciprocate help or take any of the burdens. You didn't relieve any of the stress, whatsoever just to keep hounding that person must do to get what they want and yet still say mean and nasty things about the person, is how.

The Good Doctor: Have you suddenly forgotten where I am?

Me: If you had any money like you said you, do you would be able to formulate agreement with the UN, to resolve your present issues and with your financial status, considering that you are highly valued to them.

Me: I am the scum of the earth to them, and yes, I have gained backbone. I have you, I'm humbled to the point that I put all my faith in God and will be without a place to live as of January 1.

The Good Doctor: What are you even saying Susan?

The Good Doctor: You are playing with my life, and you claim to love me?

The Good Doctor: What is money Susan?

Me: lol you played with mine and destroyed it.

The Good Doctor: Why did you write to the banister?

The Good Doctor: You are a fool, Susan.

Me: Because you didn't believe me, or even for that matter care about me. At any point you just say the words. You don't think, I don't think you mean them and what you say to me.

The Good Doctor: Sincerely speaking you are evil, have you lived in a war zone before?

Me: Yes, try life. I have nothing, no one and have been under investigation since I met you. Now I am even being followed all the time. I wish someone would just shoot me and get it over with, at this point If I am your wife, you can get what you want or need just put life insurance on me. After all it only money, true love doesn't come with a price tag.

The Good Doctor: okay I will die here in peace; thank you take good care of yourself.

Me: God is the only one I can talk to, who doesn't judge me, and he is the only one that knows I am being truthful

The Good Doctor: When I am with you, you can get whatever amount of money you want for yourself. I would save you. If I am in your position to save you and not complain about being followed about by who?

The Good Doctor: You know you are lying to yourself and not to me.

Me: He knows what I all about, and that why. He came to me twice since. God gave me something you will never understand my Good Doctor. I know what I did, I know when I die, he will be there and take me in his arms

The Good Doctor: Not when I'm left for dead, here in the in the war zone.

Me: Well, according to you, you have paper, which is what is needed. I don't have that luxury, I could and will but don't. God told me so.

The Good Doctor: You claim to have the money used to save me. When you don't. Why did you lie??? And you expect God to welcome you in his arms?

Me: Give me an address, I will send you a check. I can't do transfer and I can't do Bitcoin because the of investigation, so give me an address and I will mail it to you gladly do that LOL.

The Good Doctor: I can't give you an address you big fool.

The Good Doctor: You know my vacation process.

The Good Doctor: Don't play a fast one on me woman.

Me: May have that means, but the way to get you is all blocked welcome to Susan's new world.

The Good Doctor: Right to the banister you evil woman.

Me: Are you upset, true love doesn't call their woman evil or put them down.

The Good Doctor: Keep lying to your foolish self.

Me: I love you doctor you are so cute.

The Good Doctor: Susan, I am just tired of you right now.

The Good Doctor: If you love me, you will save me.

Me: Have a nap, must have had a hard night, smile what if I did smile, you would be happy then wouldn't you imagine if I did that, wow.

The Good Doctor: Are you continuing the process or not?

The Good Doctor: You have been so wicked to me Susan.

Me: But I love me remember.

Me: In due time.

The Good Doctor: Indeed, you act like a 2-year-old, you aren't serious one bit, beast of a woman.

Me: It's fun, I'm young at heart smile, I can laugh at my life. I can be down and out, but I still am alive.

The Good Doctor: You are going to the Bitcoin machine or not stop stressing me?

Me: No I am not on any pills, if you want to know how I feel this is the best way I can explain it to you

Sorry trying to write a poem and I don't want to forget

> From the first time I saw your face I could see a man with honor kindness and dignity.
> A doctor that cares for people and pure

I need to know you that was for sure
My heart was closed, deep buried inside
With wounds from my past, I just cannot hide
You said you loved me, you said that you cared
Never hurt me, those were your words
That you feared, lies, and betrayal you, say that you hate
But you did so to me, as you said and seal my fate
You needed a woman to get out of your mess
And played my heart, which was deep my deep duress
You needed to marry, you needed a queen
You knew from the start when you set up the scene
Someone to help you, someone a must
Made me think that you were a man I could trust
But deep inside you, you were playing a game
For I fell in love with this man that I blame
I told you I'm not a woman like most
I fall in love deep and only one host
You told me money you would not ask from me
But you knew was needed to set you free
You played with my heart you took my life away
You just needed a woman, just to get your way
My mind is clear, I know what you you've done
You heard this woman, who's now on the run
My soul and life will no longer be the same
You hurt me my dear doctor I have you to blame

The Good Doctor: I have never hurt you.

The Good Doctor: You are mistaking me for someone else babe, what is wrong with you?

The Good Doctor: I can't hurt the one I love. Stop playing this the victim here, I am suffering in this war zone.

The Good Doctor: Why are you refusing to save me now, we have gone a long way to get together babe.

The Good Doctor: Stop keeping me silent, you need to write to me more often let's trash this out once and for all?

The Good Doctor: I am tired of you talking front and back what's is your stance on us?

The Good Doctor: if you don't love me anymore say it and stop playing with my heart.

The Good Doctor: I wouldn't do this to you, but you are doing it to me!

It's unfair of you!

Me: I can't say that I always understand why some things work out and some things don't, I just try to remember that life happens the way it is meant to. Why some relationships make it and others don't. And no amount of hoping or fighting can change what it's destined to be.

Chapter Thirteen

OPEN YOUR EYES

What I do know is that out of some of my life's greatest pains has arisen some of my best triumphs. The lessons I learned through struggles are the things that have stuck with me, and while it was tough, I wouldn't change it for the world. I think back to all the times wanting something to work out the way I wanted, only to have it fall apart in front of my face. It was devastating at the time, but later, I was rewarded with something much better. It's hard to be patient, to try to have vision and see the bigger picture, when you want something so bad that it's all you can think of. It's mysterious and wonderful, amazing how the world works. If you truly step back and embrace the knowledge that was meant to be you, do it, it will always find its way to you. And to always seize the opportunities behind closed doors, no matter how much it hurts. I've had to fall to be able to rise again. I had to lose people to find better ones. I had to see the open doors because of the closed paths, and the closed doors forced me to see. I may not always have gotten everything I wanted but I've always gotten what I've needed. It's hard to open your eyes to the truth, when you're hurting and trying to understand why something happened, you realize that it's always there for you. Waiting to be understood patiently. I've never quite understood or knew why some things change while others stay the same, but I've realized that I don't have to know everything to be happy. I just must know that no matter what or how or who but no matter what happens I'll always find my way through, to a better place. And in the end, I have chosen to be happy for the pain has only taught me the lesson that showed me that the love that I was given, I was blessed with. Because in the end all and a part of me I find life is beautiful, circle of life and I always remembered that in every end there is a new beginning and that's what I look forward to.

The Good Doctor: We just have to do what my love?

The Good Doctor: I need you online more often, let's have an understanding and not going on and off my love.

The Good Doctor: I know these are trying moments, in our beautiful love and we would overcome it before Christmas comes. It hurts me so much when you don't trust me, because I trust you with everything in me.

The Good Doctor: The time you give me is too small, this is not my babe Sue, what is happening to my wife?

The Good Doctor: We need to talk and come to an understanding baby, our love is unbreakable you know this already baby.

The Good Doctor: No one can separate us baby, you can feel it in your soul.

The Good Doctor:??.

Now he ended up sending me those messages because I haven't really been talking to him much. I don't want to get back and sucked into his way of thinking. Because with all the evidence that I have seen through the police department and just in his words and actions. I have read this over several times trying to make headway or just try to understand it. It really pains me a lot, because a part of me for some reason is still in love with him. I don't understand why, considering the fact of how I was treated.

It was always about the money. It was me trying to find ways to get the money to save him. He didn't care about me at any point, or how I was or as to how I got that money. At one point I said in a flippant remark to him, well maybe I should become a prostitute, they make good money here. He said "oh how much did they make?" And just in that one statement alone shows you that he didn't care about me whatsoever, he just cared about the almighty dollar.

It also seems like it becomes a delusion, second nature to do something, to be someone, to feel that love, to feel that compassion. I'm sure you can gather that just by one of his morning rituals, where he ended up sending me a beautiful heart-wrenching-worded statement that made me feel so special. And that's one of the biggest things they try to do, is trying to make you feel special. And no matter how hard I tried to find more about him, the less I could find. And yet no matter how hard I tried to let the police know about him and what I found out, he could find it out in five minutes and yell at me for contacting the police. That to me was very confusing, very frustrating, and very contrived, but meticulously done.

Now another thing you don't really know is that he hacked my phone, when I finally stopped talking to him for the three months. About a month after that I ended up getting an abundance of emails, calls, texts, video chats, you name it, from strange men across the world. One man, believe it or not had some of the same stories, just like The Good Doctor. There was one gentleman, believe it or not, his wife and daughter died in a car crash, same number of years and he was a doctor working for the United Nations; odd right? So, I had to dig in to this one, find out what going on. That's how I ended up talking to him for a bit online.

Chapter Fourteen

THE DOPPLER EFFECTS

I'm just putting him on pause for a minute because I was doing something with some of these men that mysteriously ended up texting me, calling me, wanting to know who I was, giving me their undying love. You see, I would say most of these men, who I discovered all within a very short period of time, said they were in love with me. That's when I had to dig deeper. That's when I had to find out what's going on? Why is this happening? How many are there?

And that's what made me want to write this book. Because just from writing about The Good Doctor, I discovered how easily we can be fooled. How you can discover a man or woman or whoever they are (because this could be a child), is the one that's doing this to you. All because they want the almighty dollar. And I really don't know or, I can't say now, being a year later, whether any of these men are even real. But I just want to show you these people have only one ulterior motive. It's a way for them to get money out of you. And I'm going to repeat this:

It's a way for them to get money out of you.

And I won't stop saying this, because they don't care about you. They just want you to give them money. Money, money, money. They will say anything they want; they will tell you how much they love you, and they'll use their words to entice you, envelop you, they want you to believe in them, trust them, because all they care about is the paper. They make you feel like that paper is worthless, it has no meaning, because all these men say they have money and that they're rich. they want you to fall into their little scheme. But the longer you stay with their scheme, the deeper you get in with the money. It may start off being small amounts, doable amounts let's say, but eventually they end up getting you deeper and deeper in debt.

There is another point I want to bring up as well. How can anyone, if you really want to know or ask, be in love within a day, or just within a conversation. Especially a man, if you think about it, how can a man say he loves someone that quickly. If you look at life, to get the man to even say the words "I love you" is hard enough. But for a man to turn around and say I adore you I love you and even show emotion so extreme, how's that even possible. They use very deep, and I'll use the word contrived, words, because they want to get to their end game. They want to get your money.

Now, to show this to you, I need to continue my story. Because somehow I was getting inundated with all kinds of men from around the world, texting me, trying to video chat me, trying to swallow me, because apparently, they were my only true loves; my twin flames, my soulmates. So shall we continue? (I want you to know it almost took me 48 hours to delete all these men from my phone.) This is where you start seeing the duplications, or as I call it, the Doppler effect.

He was a Chinese gentleman., And he said hello to me, and I ended up treating him, (because I respected their ways and their culture) as one would greet a Chinese distinguished doctor. So, I in turn spoke to him with a full amount of respect and dignity, as they would in that culture. And only after about four or five texts that I sent him, he said I was one of the politest women he had ever met. And then suddenly, he said I need to tell you the truth, that is not my name. He said to me, I am a doctor in the military on a UN diplomatic mission. I kept reading. It went on to say that his wife had passed away in a tragic car accident along with his daughter. Oddly enough that was the same story that The Good Doctor gave me as well. And I said to the man, I said why the lies and deceits? And I told him all about The Good Doctor. He asked me well what's his name. I need to know his name, so I told him, and because of confidentiality and legalities, I am going to just say The Good Doctor. Well after a couple of minutes he came back with all kinds of statistics about The Good Doctor, and said he's a fraud, he's not real, stop communicating with him. I said, well the police are investigating him thoroughly right now. He says well if I could get out of here right now, he said, I would come and I would find him for you. I can do it, I have lots of money. (For some reason they have to say they have lots of money; they don't, trust me.) And then he said to me, oh can you write a letter for him, because I need someone to write a letter for me so that I can get out of the UN.

I just want to pause here for a minute. Because this gentleman here, was trying to show me that he was real. No, I didn't believe him. Nor was I even interested in him. He said he wanted to help me find this guy, said that he had the money and the means to do it. That he had a lot of pull with the United Nations. In truth you know, the old phrase once bitten, twice shy. I wasn't about to use someone just so that I could get justice for myself. It's not who I am. And that also is another ploy that they do use, they make it seem like they're going to help you with something. But the only way they're going to help you is they're going to want something from you first. And that my friend is honestly a red flag for you.

Now let us continue…

Well, I found that quite odd as well because that's exactly how it started with The Good Doctor. (Only difference was this man didn't get to me inside my heart, he just jumped in and asked me) And then he says, I will even write a letter up for you. Now this letter almost seemed like it's a footnote or something for them, to use because it was almost identical to The Good Doctor's letter. Not quite the same, but pretty close. And that to me was where I just said okay fine, NS deleted the guy off my Facebook – because he needed his fiancée to write a letter so that he could leave. However, he did do one thing that The Good Doctor didn't do, was he ended up sending me a picture of himself, along with his ID badge. And he even did a video chat with me. That was the difference, but whether he was real or fake I don't know but I was tired of this whole thing about being turned around and being used and abused.

This is when I felt the need to dig deeper, find out what is really going on here. How are there two guys, with the exact same story, claiming to be the one person that they obviously aren't? My inquisitive nature had to find out. I needed to know how bad this was. How far would these people go? Let's face it you don't know if it's a man or a woman.

The Doppler effect.

So, I do want you to know one thing, and it's kind of a scary thing to know. That there are at least one in ten cons on the Internet that are claiming to be someone who, first off, they're not, and secondly, are going to claim to fall deeply in love with you and use words that are going to make you feel like you're on top of the world.

The reason why you're going to feel on top of the world is because of the one chemical that's in your body, that's going to make you or break you. And you know what that chemical is. I gave you full information on that. And I'll tell you, you feel like you're on the best ride of the world when that happens. You feel so alive, so energized, so beautiful that somehow, we've got some comfort and compassion from someone who's only there to take your money. And you must come to some point of self-realization in yourself that this is not real.

Chapter Fifteen

GETTING AHOLD
OF YOURSELF

And I know for a fact that it's not easy, because I'm still having difficulty dealing with my feelings towards this gentleman, The Good Doctor. Part of me is still in love with this man, and that's something I don't understand. That's something I don't know how to get past, in a way. But I do know he was a fake and a fraud. I'm going to grab ahold of my life, and I'll tell you what I did to be able to do that. But it's not just being able to grab ahold of yourself but it's being able to grab ahold of your reality.

I also believe that it's truly important for you to understand the steps that he took and how he took them, to give you signs to understand why this is happening to you, why you're feeling certain things and I'm hoping before you get too deep in with someone like I did to be able to save yourself the grief the misery, the loneliness, and the torment that you're going to feel along with all the humiliation and embarrassments of all the things that a con does to you.

The first thing I want to talk about is obviously the introduction with the con. What is it that's causing you to talk to this person?

You're going to have to analyze yourself because obviously there is more bad people on the Internet than good ones. Their intentions aren't what they seem. I want to stress that; their intentions aren't what they seem. The first thing that attracts you to an individual obviously is looks. Something about their looks gets you into them. And if it's not the looks it's their position or their title that they claim to have; what they're doing, what their job is. Mine just happened to be a neurologist who worked for the United Nations on a humanitarian mission, and he was also chief of staff for them. So, he had a lot of bells and whistles attached to his name. That plus his looks; I thought he was one of the hottest looking guys I've ever seen and here he was texting me, a 63-year-old woman. Wow I thought to myself this is kind of nice that this guy even shows an interest in me to even want to be my friend. The other thing that attracted me to him was the fact that he was a widow for six years, because I felt I had some common ground with him. He had gone through the same experience as me in a way because we don't expect death to just happen. It's not our mindset it's not how we look at life and regardless every death is done in an instant. But it's the emotional impact that it has on us that causes us to seek out people with some commonality, who relate to that factor as well.

So, their first step obviously is to get your attention, by using looks, or a job title. The next step is their wording, how they talk to you and what they say to you. And this is how The Good Doctor ended up talking to me in the beginning. He told me I was beautiful, that he had never seen a vision as lovely as me. I replied and said that's a very old picture you got there I look nothing like that now. At the time I was still 50 pounds overweight, plus I didn't like the way I looked. But he said he didn't care what I looked like now, he said he was connected to me in a way, that somehow our meeting was fate and that it was meant to be. I rebutted again and said I was not a normal type of woman; I have a different mindset. I have false teeth, I have arthritis; I started naming off everything that was wrong with me in honesty. But that didn't seem to fizz on him; he said, I don't care what you look like on the outside it's the person that's inside of you that I like, and I've fallen for. Well, those words kind of make you feel good about yourself, don't they, but in those words even though they are simple, very beautiful words mind you, it's the simplicity of those words that ends up getting your dopamine levels up. Yes, that is a very important point I'm making here, it's the words they are using that cause your dopamine levels to rise.

That's why it's important for you to know about this chemical inside yourself; a lot of people aren't aware that this is something that causes you to be happy, causes you to get excited, causes you to have the drive you desire to get what you want to be who you are and live your life, basically in a dream world to a point. I know it sounds amazing and a thrill for you now if you just want to give your money away to someone and experience that, go right ahead but I'd say you're foolish because they won't stop. As you can see by the conversation above, they are relentless. That's how a narcissist works by the way, they work on your love, your emotions, your fear for their safety. You want to save them, you want to do something good, and they want to make you feel good by doing that. But it doesn't stop there because I could guarantee if I sent that $200,000 to him, I'll end up with another letter that's going to ask for $400,000 because it always seems to duplicate. There isn't an end; you'll never see them, and I want to stress the word never because you'll never ever see them. There will always be something else. I do remember when I did send the money for the consignment box; I told him I was worried, I said I'm just waiting for the other shoe to drop. And it dropped big time.

And that's the next phase that they do, is they try to use fear against you. The way he used the fear obviously is in that last bout of conversation over the last month. He didn't like the fact that

I wasn't spending time with him daily because that way he'd get me back in his clutches, make me feel the remorse the sorrow, the love, the connection. And the true love because in your heart you feel like you're truly in love with that person. His words are how he gets you hooked on him (or her obviously because I know this has happened to men as well as women). I spoke to a gentleman who was a high official in the government, and he was conned in the six-digit figures. He felt like a fool, just like me because he believed in that person. I can honestly say to you that your heart will be torn if you continue with an individual that is doing this to you. I am telling you from the bottom of my heart I want to save you the grief, the pain, and the hurt that you will feel because I'll tell you right now the police have been involved with my case for the last five to six months, going on six months and still with all the knowledge that I've learned from the police department and the fact that they can't even find this gentleman, even though they're using cyber teams and every piece of information they possibly can, in the end they're still not going to find him. They know how to use the Internet against everything.

You see what happens is if it's in Canada where I am, let's say they can just go to the person's place. Or even in the United States, they can have them speak with the individuals there, which they did in my case. But then that just led to another lead which took them to another place which was the Netherlands, to a gentleman there that she had sent the money to after she received it. Now one of the things that I do know from what The Good Doctor had told me was that she works for the United Nations and because of the secrecy and the security measures she can't divulge that she works for the United Nations, not even to the police, because apparently the terrorists will find out. See that's how they use their excuses; that's how they make up things so that you have no recourse against them, from their words. How do you combat that? Do you want to be a party to that? I can't stress it enough that the feelings you have are your only failing; it's a one-sided love affair, because even though that person on the other end is sending you information as you can see this last conversation was just within the past month.

Now another thing that they do it's because they're so good with the Internet and I mean everything of mine was compromised. My social insurance number, my bank accounts, and all my money obviously and then some which ended up putting me into a consumer proposal which I thought I'd never have to do. Because I'd never had to worry about money before in my life. I was one of the most stable people out there. I was always helping others because I cared about people; like I said before if someone needed help with rent, food, clothing, shelter whatever, I helped. I just have that personality. I have had people walk up to me when I've gone for walks, that I didn't know, start telling me about their whole life stories. I guess I just have that kind of face, that lets people know that I'm there for them and that I have a good ear to listen with. And a lot of my friends and family have told me that I walk around with my heart on my sleeve, that I have a heart, only because I care about people. Are you one of those people? So, you see, anyone can be vulnerable to this whether you're on disability or like me I'm on a widow's pension only, but I was always frugal with my money and like I said I'm not a materialistic person I don't have a materialistic bone in my body quite honestly so I'm a very simple person. Or you could have money like I did at one point and then lose it all to that person, that you thought you were in love with. Because The Good Doctor got into my head, and he took my heart, which I don't give out freely, never have.

My husband's friends all tried to hit on me but I never accepted it. I loved my husband too much, or what I thought was love at the time, because I got married to him when I was 18. But we met when I was 13 and he was 12, he was almost a year younger than me. And we didn't have sexual relations until I was 17 and a half, when I ended up getting pregnant with my first daughter. He asked me to marry him back then, prior to her birth, but I had the foresight to say no, I wasn't going to be pregnant and get married so that he could use that as an excuse for a fight. Funny though because we never really fought in our whole marriage, I didn't like fighting. And because of that I didn't like arguments whatsoever.

Which leads to another point of how they get the dopamine levels to rise. What happens is they start using words to entice you. To give you the infatuation of love, to start with. You do become infatuated with the individual. And to me I even said to him I think I'm just infatuated with you right now. It only took him a day or so to tell me that he was in love with me. I did not comprehend that portion of it at that point. I couldn't see how someone who just talked to someone via text on the Internet could love someone at that point. But from what I've read they say that men know who they love regardless it's not something that they can control from my readings, because I did do a lot of research on this to try and find out how someone can manipulate you. It's easier to manipulate someone and be a womanizer or a man-izer I guess I'm not sure how that's really done or if that's the proper term. But it's easier when you're face to face with someone. However, they use systematic words that cause your dopamine levels to increase. There are books you can buy so that you can find out how they do this. I ended up buying quite a few of them because I was very much into trying to figure out how I got derailed, I guess is a good term.

Now in saying that to increase your dopamine levels when you're in a relationship with someone does it. At some point you start caring more about that person, but they still want to make sure that they keep your attention. How did they do that? It's quite simple, first you get the person's attention, and even if they're just infatuated with that individual, the way to increase it is to give that push and pull feeling. And what I mean by a push and pull feeling is they want to get to into your emotions. They want you to want them, but then they want to take it away from you a little and back off a bit. Just so that you can and will only think of that individual, until you become obsessed with the individual to the point where you're thinking about them 24/7. Quite ingenious, but quite simple as well.

Sometimes I wonder if God has a sense of humor, or bigger than he can possibly think of, because of some of the ways that people's emotions are affected immensely. So, in looking at the end that sensor your POV you must consider everything that goes on. And that will increase your dopamine levels traumatically.

You see what he did at one point with me was he blocked me if you remember me saying so. What did that do to me? That made me start obsessing about him, that I needed to talk to him, that I wanted to explain myself. It affected my emotions. It basically made me run closer to him than further away. So, in that context, they're using fear of loss. Because when they first start chatting with you, they make you feel so wonderful, they put you on a pedestal so quickly without you even realizing or having knowledge that you're being pulled into their space. That makes you want and strive more just to get closer to them. You want that high. It's funny, there was one time when I was talking to him or texting him, I should say, quite honestly, I consider sometimes texting as talking, so please bear with me. But in saying that it's an odd thing because your perception gets warped. At one point in our conversations, I told him I felt like I was high. Because that's how he made me feel, because he changed my emotions. It was so different than with my late spouse, and without realization I ended up falling deeper and deeper in love with The Good Doctor.

So now you can see how crucial it is to understand a small part of what they use to achieve their end game. Basically because that's how I look at it, as a game. To them it's all about the money, it's not whether they're affecting an individual. Because as he said to me, if you notice throughout all our conversations is that I would do nothing to hurt you. I only want to help you I love you we're soulmates you name it. And by saying all these things to you in turn start believing it, in honesty I was on the phone almost 24/7. I would be asleep, and I would hear my phone ding. it's like I needed that ding, I needed that high, I needed to talk to him and see what he had to say to me. You get so involved and engrossed with everything about that person, and the funny part is I still to this day don't know a lot about this person. He still plays the role of a Good Doctor who is in the United Nations, under a diplomatic contract for humanity. He was a humanitarian (so he said) and cared for people, saved people, and helped people in a desperate situation, a war zone of all things. And part of you starts fearing for that individual as well and that's our next point.

Using that loss of fear

Now the way I look at it is, first they make you feel like you're beautiful and you get to a point where you start loving yourself. They want you loving yourself, because you can't really love someone else until you truly love yourself. And a part of me didn't love myself, so he made me love me. And then The Good Doctor decided to pull back a little bit, to let me see what it would be like without him in my life. But after a day and a half he was back on with me, got me where he wanted me. Then he decided to add fear.

He started telling me about the terrorists infiltrating the hospital and that he lost some of his good colleagues due to terrorists. In his words he showed sadness and remorse, but he also showed fear for himself and his own safety. He told me once that he was cowered in a corner, that the terrorists got in and he was afraid, thinking he was next to be killed. He also told me once where a friend of his had to go, was transferred to where the actual war was and his friend, his colleague, got killed. He also told me that they got bombed and he was running from one location to another and ended up tripping and spraining his ankle. I tried to use words to console him. I told him I was kissing his foot when he went to bed and rubbing it and doing everything I could, being his little nurse Sue. And he liked it when I called myself nurse Sue because he started calling me nurse Sue. He also told me that they were pillaged by the terrorists, and they had no food left, they had taken everything, that he had no food to eat. And that the military was trying to find a way to find more rations for them. A lot of times he'd have to eat pork and beans because there was nothing else to eat. So, then your thoughts are plumbing levels, they change again, now you're thinking oh my God, my dear darling doctor is suffering so much and lacking so much from being where he is. So, then you start to think of ways to do what you can to help them. This is one reason that I started the process of trying to write a letter, so that he can get his vacation leave. My thought levels kept changing, increasing, expanding, and that's going to happen to you too. And these are things you must consider in the process of what's going on. You need to be aware of what's happening because each event that they talk about with you in detail, the detailed conversations they have with you about their emotions, is what increases your emotions and causes the dopamine levels to increase.

And because of all this, it started stressing me out. I started not eating, I felt bad for him, and my appetite decreased tremendously. Most of the times I would have a hardboiled egg for breakfast and just that with a tea and lemon. Yes, I did love my tea with lemon, and I still do. But it's small things that build up to big things, and the big thing I'm talking about is your bank account. One of the things I didn't mention to you was he asked me if I had any money. At first, I said I don't have much, I have enough to live on, but that's about it. He made me feel that I needed to save him, that it was my God-given right and my duty to help a fellow man, to save him from the deadly war.

So now, let's just look at what they've done so far, here on this picturesque equation that they've done to you. Because now you're sitting there thinking okay, I've got feelings for this person now. I need to do something, anything I can do to try and help them. And that's how I ended up writing the first letter to the United Nations to pay for his vacation leave. Pretty smart, isn't it, and yet it's simple in the same process.

It doesn't stop there; the amounts end up increasing and increasing each time. You keep doing what they want and get to the point that they think you can get money at the drop of the hat. But even though you keep sending money, one thing stays constant, you never get to bring him to you and you can't save them, so to speak. It's only to get the money off you. And that's what scares me for you, when someone basically invades your heart, you're not thinking with your mind anymore, you're not thinking logically, your dopamine levels are taking you from thinking logically to emotionally. You must recapture your own thoughts, capture them, use your gut. Because I'll tell you my gut did tell me at times, don't do this, it's wrong, stop what you're doing. But because of my dopamine levels that I had at the time, it made me bypass that feeling. If your gut says no, listen to it. I know you're going to feel good; I know you're going to want to build on that feeling, capture it, encapsulate it, enjoy it. Oh my God, I mean to me it was a rush, and truly I was on a high. But at some point, you've got to come to the realization prior to losing all your money, prior to going into debt like I had. These are the things that happen. I'm talking about reality here, and that's going to be my next part.

Reality

One of the things I discovered from all this is that, as I got tired of looking at the Internet to find someone to love for real. Yes, people do fall in love off the Internet. Recently there was a woman in England who fell in love with a man in the United States, but they were FaceTiming each other, talking to each other, and believe it or not they got married over the Internet. So yes, it can happen, yes there is an odd chance, and I underline the word odd. In truth, the odds of finding your true soulmate online is slim to none. If they start asking you for money, that should already tell your gut no. Because you don't want to go there, because it doesn't end there, it just keeps going. They just keep taking from you, and then there's always another obstacle that you must go through to get an inch closer to what you think is going to be real. I've done a lot of soul-searching to try and figure out how someone can captivate an individual through the Internet. How can someone feel and love through the Internet?

Chapter Sixteen

FINDING A WAY

I just said that, and I want to explain something to you as well. I met many gentlemen on the Internet after the The Good Doctor. And I've grown very fond of many of them. I even started falling for some of them; I needed to find out how The Good Doctor did this, I needed to know how it worked. How they did it to show the pattern. I knew from what happened with The Good Doctor that yes, I was manipulated, and used. It had nothing to do with love, it was what they could gain from me. They all seem to say they love me, and want me, but they all did the same thing, they played me.

Once I did break it off with The Good Doctor, I said, yes, I do deserve love in my life. I should be happy. If nothing else The Good Doctor taught me that I too should have someone in my life. When I tried talking to other men on dating sites, somehow The Good Doctor knew. I was afraid The Good Doctor would start to yell and scream, and carry on, through email or an encrypted message through someone on my phone, because he did it before just when I was talking to someone. He even sent a clip via Hangouts of all places, showing me one of the conversations I had through a text with that individual. And this was after the police were involved. So, I kind of know he got into my phone, my phone is compromised at this point. He even sent an email via my grandson's girlfriend's phone number, who texted me about something. I went to put her number in my phone and there was a message from him, hidden underneath the message.

This is what it said: it had the girlfriend's phone number; underneath it said The Good Doctor; below that, it said government; then it had The Good Doctor's email address. Nope, Sorry if I did wrong, here's my email, and then it showed my email.

> I sent you some messages, not sure if you read them, may have scared you off, was just me, but want to try thanking you for being so nice to me. I don't like putting certain things on Facebook.

So, you see these are indications that my phone was compromised. I've even had messages across the top of my screen, and I knew it was from him just by the way he wrote them. I can't remember them offhand, but he was taunting me for sure. He wanted to let me know that he could still get to me somehow, regardless of what I do or say or how many times I try to block him. I block him, but he's just always there. Always trying to get me back to where he had me, so that I would move mountains and find more money to save him. It got to the point where I became exhausted from the search and anguish and frustration. I was starting to be very disillusioned and scared.

And when it came to the $200,000 right at the beginning there when I said there's no way I can get that money. He said, well you can get the money. I know you can. And then he started to kind of threaten me in certain ways trying to force me to get the money. What I mean by threatening he knew about my family, my grandkids, and how much they meant to me. This happened when he wanted me to get the consignment box too, and I had to get money. But when I didn't have enough in the bank, he says to me, you can do it, you can get this money, you can do anything, you live in a rich country. And then he started asking me questions about how's my daughter-in-law and how's my granddaughter. He gave her name, and he said, I can get to you anytime I want. Then I said to him, well, come do it yourself then, come do it face to face, bring the knife, and kill me right here. I'm not scared of you, but because of you I'm not allowed to see my grandchildren, my family has disowned me. So, then what do you do, I said to him, you're not going to show up anyway. If you're going to do it you might as well come yourself, don't get one of your henchmen to do. Quite honestly, I feared him, threating my family. I didn't care what he might have done to me, but you don't hurt my family. I don't care if they've disowned me or whatever but that you don't threaten me using them. So, they can get quite nasty just so you know, and regardless of what happens you got to keep moving forward.

So, let's recap some of the things just for a moment.

1: The pictures they send, you must be careful with that.

2: Your own chemistry is your worst enemy, because of the dopamine in your system. It affects your emotions and builds and one of the things I didn't tell you was

3: I was meditating quite a bit and he knew it. I was meditating a lot and sometimes I would do three or four a day maybe five. It might have been a little excessive, but I still did that.

4: What you eat. I ate a lot of eggs for starters. That also affects your dopamine levels, but the reason I was eating eggs was it was one of the things that helped me lose my weight. It's a diet I made myself just so you know. I was also feeling better about myself because

5: I did a lot of walking. So, I had many things that were increasing my dopamine levels inside my system. I didn't know that's what was doing that to me.

6: Obviously the words that he used, you can tell by some of the information that he did send me.

7: Causing friction between the two of you. Where he either doesn't talk to you for days on end or fights with you and causes you to get agitated, then uses sexting to make up with you.

These are all factors in what he or she does, because you really don't know who it is that you're talking to. They do take things away from you, and one of the biggest things he took away from me was my dignity, and my family really because now I'm to a point where I must be out of the basement apartment at the end of this month. And that is a fact that we all must deal with. At times regardless of what we do for family, with what we must do to help them, we do out of love. And if that's love, I don't know because I can't leave a man behind. It's not me, it's not who I am, or what I'd want to be.

You must look at every single angle of what's happening to you and I'm trying to use my heart here to talk to you, because sometimes family will say things you may not realize what they're trying to do. In one way some will feel compassion to ease you from this crime. It is a crime; I mean it's a $60 million business nowadays, they make a ton of money. I was told by the police department that my chances of even recouping 1 cent from this guy is pretty much zero. Those aren't good odds for me for you or anyone else out there dealing with someone you believe is real. There are also websites on the Internet you can go to just see pictures and names of cons. Just type in a web search and look if you have any doubts whatsoever, please look and see.

There's nothing worse than having your life taken from under you; your security, your values, your beliefs. He has made me deceive people by omitting information, not saying what's going on, hiding the fact that I'm even speaking with him. And there's one other thing that he did that I didn't mention yet. He starts taking you away from the media. Doesn't want you to watch the news. Doesn't want you on Facebook whatsoever. Anything having to do with media or talking to someone was a definite no-no. Partially because he kept telling me, well it's the terrorists making that information up. He couldn't stand it when I was on the Internet checking things out.

He didn't like the fact that I spoke with the girl who I sent the money to (the one he claimed to work for the United Nations). He called her a liar and a cheat, and yet under the same breath said that she worked for the United Nations. So, he was backtracking a lot when I was doing these things and trying to find answers quickly. So, you really must watch yourself, please take some of my words to heart. Because, if you don't, it's going to change your life for the worst. And even though I still wasn't fully getting everything I needed for him, because even though I paid almost $100,000 for the consignment box and other things. I had to do which I forgot to mention as I sold most of my jewelry, the jewelry I was going to give my grandchildren and my kids and I'm not proud of that whatsoever now. All they get for me now is a memory. Because now I have nothing and no one.

He didn't like anyone with baggage, and he wanted to make sure that I would have nothing and no one. Even though he said he loved family and children, does someone do that to family and children ever? Is that how one should behave? The answer is no, and I found out the why too late for me, but in a sense it's not too late, if you're just starting off on an Internet relationship, if you haven't given them any money, you need to look at everything and think before you act or say.

One of the other things he always used to do was when I said I was going to do something he made me promise to him. Because when one promises something to someone you follow through, I'm not sure if you're the same way or not, but if you are then you're in trouble. Don't ever promise instead, you should make him promise to you. Turn it around, put the onus on them. Find a way because if he expects you to find a way to get the money then obviously, he has a way to get the money as well. If they say they have money, yet they are asking you for it, you know the truth inside, okay, save yourself and your dignity. I think that's the best advice I can possibly give you on that. You must determine to yourself what needs to be done, what you need to do for you, without changing who you are, without having to change your personality, and one of the biggest keys to knowing that this is a con. Plus I would think the fact that he doesn't want you to tell anyone. Because if you're not telling anyone what you're doing and what he's asking of you, you know it's a con.

Chapter Seventeen

REPEAT, IT'S VIRTUAL

One of the things I did realize from The Good Doctor was I was very lonely and just existing in life. I wanted to find someone for me. Now I was having people off my Facebook still contacting me wanting to date me and talk to me blah blah blah. I ended up coming to the conclusion recently, that virtual is just that, it's virtual it's not real. You must look at it in a different mindset. I know we long for someone, and I know we really want something true to happen to us. To give us some peace and comfort. But through all this yes, I did discover that I want someone for me and how does one obtain it in today's society. It's not like a 63-year-old goes out all over the place all the time to meet men. It's not who I am, especially since I was married for 45 Years, a widow for five.

So, you must resort two what you have and continue. I then started to you the Internet. In this process, in doing so, the Internet ironically, I made a profile with the help of my daughter and her sister-in-law, (who said you get local men on there) I ended up going on plenty of fish. They said you know what, there's a lot of decent guys out there, it's a good safe website go on. So, I went on the site and I'm telling you there is like hundreds of men on this site. I can't even tell you how many, but decent no, I've deleted men they wanted to get to know me (Not know me, if you get my drift). Very overwhelming, very hard to try and figure out just from words, pictures, and the little spiels about themselves, who they are.

Now I did accept quite a few, just to find out you know and feel for myself how it works. In the process ironically, there was a picture of a doctor, who said he was 63 and wanted to get to know me. I sent a hello and we chatted for a little bit, and he asked if I wanted to go to a different web format so that we can talk privately. Now one of the things, I didn't do which I should have wise listen to the rules and safety. I disregarded it, but in the process, I was speaking with this so-called doctor, I was completely forthright and honest with him. I told him I was conned I told him I was completely broke, strapped, no money at these points no family really. Anyway, I told him the absolute truth. I told him I was writing a book because I wanted to help people who are going through the same thing, and him being a doctor, I even said it was the dopamine levels. And he seemed quite fascinated about that, then somehow my words got to him, because I was talking from my heart about what happened to me. And suddenly, he said to me I want to tell you something. I said fine go right ahead. Then he sends me a picture of himself. It was a young lad in an underprivileged country, and he wanted money not because he really needed it, but because he wanted to buy himself a better surround sound system for his computer. He even sent the information to me of the thing he wanted to buy. I was flabbergasted, but before I even did that I kind of knew he was a con, because I looked up the number that he gave me that he sent me when we started chatting. He said he was a doctor from Toronto. I thought it was kind of odd because I was looking at the phone number. And because of that I have learned quite a bit. I become more aware of whom I'm speaking with, just like you're going to have to do. I told this boy, that he was hurting many women by what he was doing. That it was wrong. He said he knew it was, said he needed the money and had no other way of getting the money. I tried to get through to him. I know he's not going to change, but it's going to take people like you and me and all our strength together to save yourself.

This is something I thought you should know; they are real people that they use. I looked up the name online to see if there was such a doctor, and there is a doctor in Toronto with the same name. But the odd thing that got me was the number. It started with an 805-area code and when you look up that area code it talks about scammers. Do and be diligent about this before you even give one red cent to someone, if you have that urge to do it. Or at least realize that there are more scams out there, more people that are just in for what they can get out of it, their monetary values not yours. Because in honesty they don't love you. I'm sorry to say it, but they don't, it's all a façade, make belief, because virtual is not real.

And I was also talking to another scammer on the site, yeah, there's lots of them I think it's only one in nine are real, for the real true reason. I found out that who he was, wasn't who he said he, that his name was different than the picture. I ended up doing a pictures reverse search which you can do as well. And this is what I told this scammer. I know you might not talk to me again but, I just want to give you a little advice. I want you to start believing in yourself, to stop hiding your identity because, the only person you are fooling is yourself. It doesn't matter what others think of you, it does matter what you think of yourself, so, start so start believing in yourself, because once you know who you are inside you can grow, live life, be happy and live your wildest dreams. Don't let others choose your path, live for you please. I say this with conviction and compassion to start loving yourself, please. I hope you do read this because I care for you that much, please. What others think about you doesn't matter, it's what you believe in yourself that matters. Now the reason why this gentleman said this to me was because he was ashamed of who he was and didn't want women to want him for something else other than for him. (Whether this is true or just a lie to hide his identity I don't know) That's what he's claiming to me. They are words again, it's not truth, it's not fact, without seeing the whites of the eyes you can't distinguish the difference. They all say they love you; they want you, and only you. They want to take care of you, that they know all about you, but they don't. They are words. And the harsh truth is the more I dig the more I find. Because of my analytical and logical side of my brain, I need to know how things work, I need to figure out the whys, what causes them to do this. I know there are good men out there on the Internet. Any way you look at it the cons using others identities are causing those people's lives to be tainted because of these scammers let's face it, that's what they are. It's their so-called pride at stake. They need to figure out how they can get something and manipulate you, just to line their pockets. It even gets to the point where they want you to do things that you know in your heart are wrong illegal. They don't care if they put your life at risk if they get money from you. can So do take to heart every word I say, because I am giving it to you from my heart.

No man or a woman really, because there's been many men that have been conned too, that I've spoken with as well. The cons only want to abuse you physically and mentally really, it's you are fighting with yourself and that's what we have to get past.

I wrote a poem about the man I thought I was in love with.

From the first time I saw your face I could see
A man of honor kindness and dignity
A doctor that cares for people and more
I needed to know you that was for sure
My heart was closed deep buried inside
With wounds from my past, I just wanted to hide

You said the that you love, me you said that you cared
Never hurt me or use me, your words that you fared
Lies and betrayals you say that you hate
But you did so to me, as you sealed my fate
You needed a woman to get out of your mess
And played with my heart which was deep in duress
You needed to marry, you needed a queen
You knew from the start when you set up the scene
Someone to help you, that someone a must
Made me think that it that you were a man I could trust
But deep down inside you, were playing a game
Before I fell in love with this man that I blame
I told you I'm not a woman like most
I fell deep in love and only one host
You played with my heart, you took my life away
You just needed a woman, just to get your way
You told me money you would not ask for me
But knew was needed to set you free
My mind is clear, and I know what you've done
You hurt this woman who's now on the run
My soul and life will no longer be the same
You hurt me dear doctor, I have you to blame

Chapter Eighteen

THE OTHER CONS

PART ONE

By now I'm sure that you can understand certain things that have happened to me. And how it can happen to you. I have been talking to several men online, seven to be exact. It's quite amazing how the duplication works, is created by these men. I'm going to number them, and you'll see certain repeating with each one.

Man Number 1 is a guy on a rig very sweet at first, loving and caring as a matter of fact. I don't think he's ever tried to be mean to me. He said he understood me, I told him everything that happened to me with the con from the beginning. I even said to him why don't you just walk away, leave me alone. I don't want anyone else getting hurt over this. He insisted on being my friend, well with him he was always kind and compassionate. Wanted me to be his friend couple times over, but then one day he wanted a card. I said I have no money to give, they all have their own unique style. I guess you could say, this one (just like the other cons) said all that he was interested in was to love me. That he finished his contract and was going to come to me and was supposed to be here in December (never asked for money again). I've known him for I guess a couple weeks after The Good Doctor, and we have been chatting for about 6 months. Because of what happened to me you could say I was on the rebound man, someone to take some of the pain away from me.

Oddly enough, the day came where he was packing up getting ready to leave and getting ready to go to the airport. The strangest thing happened, he got stopped at customs. And what happens, I get a text on Hangouts, it said something like this, ma'am you're your partner has been stopped at the border. He's been detained because he has illegal drugs, and there is a fine that has to be paid prior to him being able to leave. Well, I was mortified, when I heard that, being a Christian, you'd think that he wouldn't do something like that to start with. He seemed to be a well-rounded individual, always showed honesty in his words, his actions. He'd send me little clips and stuff like that, tell me what he was up to and what he was doing. Even video chatted and sent pictures of himself to me. But here I find out that he's carrying illegal drugs, wow. I said, well apparently, he says he's got lots of money in the bank, get him to pay it. Well ma'am he's being detained until this fine is paid; he cannot access his funds. How convenient (I thought) right, they're asking me for money and wanting me to send it by bitcoin. That's not going to happen, I'm very broke because of the previous con. I thought for sure I was going to have someone that cared about me, was honest with me and was going to be there for me. And basically, I said, you know I hope everything goes well with him, and this is a conversation that transpired with man Number 1.

So here goes the conversation now apparently this isn't man Number 1, it's the security guard (con) or whatever you want to call them.

Security Guard: Ma'am your fiancée Mr. Number 1 is just a good man, and he said he is willing to refund that back to you as soon as he can get out of here.

Me:? Why isn't he out then, why isn't he on a plane, if you want money, I have none.

Me: Can't get more

Me: I turned everything to stone.

Me: So, I'm dead.

Me: Tell Number 1 I loved him, but please I'm done.

Security Guard: Ma'am, if you say that then there is no way I can be of help here anymore.

Me: lol yeah there is, he says he has money let him give it to you.

Me: He destroyed my life. I can't pay back what I borrowed, and there were people that did know what happened to me.

Security Guard: Ma'am, he says he is refunding all that back to you as soon as he can get home.

Me: lol yeah, that what the conned that took me for, everything, that I am**** ** myself. (fear of loss) it's done sweetheart. I don't live, I can't live like this anymore. I'm afraid to get go back to my sons. I am alone. I have no one left no money.

Security Guard: Ma'am I'm sorry about that.

Me: Today, I always lived for today, but now I have nothing left, tell him I'm sorry, but I think I won't see tomorrow.

Me: Tell him I love him, though in a bizarre way, I love him me. I have no hope.

Me: Merry Christmas.

Me: There was a time I couldn't walk away, but my strength has given me the courage to do that however I need my weakness to do that ironic huh.

Me: Funny it's strength that saves us, it's our pride that kills us, been living I am in my car for days now. I just have the battery and a little gas smile.

NOTE: That was a lie, I was in Toronto at Sue's place, and she was right next to me when I was typing. I knew I was just being played for money.

Security Guard: Ma'am, your fiancée says as soon as he gets out of here, he was going to get you a house and refund you everything that they were scam done, as we are going to try and go after those scammers' ma'am.

Me: doesn't matter really does it. I'm running and on low here, I'm real, I'm truly alone.

Me: Never thought my last days would be like this but that is life.

Security Guard: Ma'am, getting the documents closed as we are talking about hard drugs here, and not just being detained this is against the law, and you know that, ma'am, if he got hold of $1050 for that the documents will be closed out. This may lead to an international re arrest and be detained all over again. Ma'am. But I'm sorry if you are fed up, there is nothing I can do either, rather than turn off his phone and have it kept somewhere he can't get it when he is fully out.

NOTE: Once again, fear of loss, once again they are asking me to save them. It's a way of them getting to you. My friend Sue and I sat there on the couch talking about what was going on, how they play with your feelings. I on the other hand was furious about the whole thing. I figured I would look like someone with nothing left in life, to just give up. If you knew me, I don't give up.

Me: Funny you say that he had to be on first plane out, but there is always something, isn't there. LOL, when one has strength to walk away, something I never been able to do. I have nothing no way, I can't get $2,500 US lol. I'll be dead before you know it OK. I have nothing for it even, nothing left for gas to keep me warm. I don't know what Number 1 did, but I don't have nothing else. Nothing I can do, sorry, but tomorrow is not coming for me, say goodbye OK. I can't help me, let alone Number 1.

Me: And I love him, I must walk away and be a speck now on this universe.

Me: Simply, I can save me now, so I can't save him I'm sure he can find someone to help him. I did all I could do, he will have to find someone else or get a loan, but I done I can't, I admit defeat.

Me: Sadly I saved many, but no one can save me now.

Me: Plus, surely to God someone else can help him for a week-old woman who is tired cant. I could hope to fall asleep quickly and can't take the cold.

Me: Guess I the evil queen, but when you know you have no other recourses, what does one do, bye my love.

Security Guard: Ma'am, your fiancée wishes to talk to you on the phone, and I'm only going to allow him to do that for a few minutes.

They try a connection but for some reason it fails, go figure right.

Me: Bad connection, sorry but I am going from Sue's, been parked in her visitor parking.

Security Guard: okay ma'am, he is going to call you later.

NOTE: Never got the call.

Me: She's the only one that knows what I am going through.

Security Guard: I'm handing the phone over to your fiancée for some minutes ma'am.

Me: OK.

Sue ended up taking the phone because I was having difficulties then I really didn't want to talk anymore I was done with it. Now Sue played along with what I was doing, you can see they had no sympathy at all, and she fought to get some kind of a reaction from them. This is what Sue said:

Sue: This is Sue's friend; she is really upset about all this.

Sue: Stop asking her for money, she has none and no way of getting any.

Sue: She feels like she would rather be dead, she can't even pay her own bills due on 30th of this month.

Sue: She is a mess.

Sue: She feels bad for Number 1, she loved him, but can't help him anymore, her heart is breaking in front of me.

Sue: For a moment she's with me safe, but she wants to leave. I'm doing everything I can to help her because I love her, and I don't want to see her hurt like this anymore.

Sue: it is our Christmas time; I won't let you stress her out anymore.

Sue: She really loves this guy called Number1, and it pains her so much that she can't help she is crying, and her nerves are shot, and her soul is dying, please send some good news soon.

Security Guard: I am sorry ma'am, if there is any other way for me to help, I would have done that myself, as the man in question Number 1 sounds so nice and honest, and if it was in my place to do all this, I would, he should have been on a plane before this minute ma'am.

Sue: There must be a way to find someone else he knows to help.

Sue: Cannot be his only help, she is my best friend. I love her so. I believe she will kill herself if I let her leave here, where is number one you, said he would give her him the phone.

Security Guard: Sweetheart, it's me Number 1.

Sue: Hi.

(Apparently) Number 1: Darling, I know you must have go through a lot trying to Get Me Out of here.

Number 1: My love, I'm really sorry for stressing you this much just to Get Me Out.

Number 1: Just want you to know I feel your pain here, and just can't wait to be with you sweetie, if there is any way you can Get Me Out of here, please… do I don't like it here, just want to be with you my love,

Sue: You must have some can help you. I have nothing else; I can't do, she is living in my car since Monday

Number 1: Starting to tell Sue, I really appreciate her for assisting you on this as what her to know that I will refund every amount she spent on this and even with interest if she wants.

Sue: You were the one thing that kept you going was you.

Number 1: Darling, just want you to be with to be with you.

Number 1: I'm eager sweetheart just feel bad right now knowing you are not fine do breaks my heart.

Me: Well, if you are counting on me, I'm sorry, I have nothing, this may be the last time we talked. I can't guarantee tomorrow, sweetheart just know I love you with all my heart. I do hope you stay happy love you

Number 1: Honey please do try.

Number 1: Sweetheart, I really want to be with you darling, don't leave me now that I need you the most, please my love.

(Sent a batch of emojis crying)

Me: I can't answer that sweetheart I don't know God will judge, he only one other than a real judge.

Me: I love you.

(Sent said emoji face)

Me: I sent a heart.

Number 1: You know I love you more than my life, more my wife. (Sent emoji rose)

Me: Would send a picture, but at kind of look bad.

Number 1: it's you I want sweetheart.

Number 1: Need you more now than ever.

(Sent an emoji koala hugging a bear)

Me: I don't want you to Remember Me this way OK.

Me: My teddy bear's mob thank you.

Number 1: My heart, I just want to be with you, my love.

Me: I want you, but don't seem to be getting anywhere so I stuck.

Number 1: Honey, they just told me my phone will be taken from soon me.

Me: my life is at an all-time low.

Number One: I'm not allowed to make use of my phone.

Number One: Darling, please try your best, and see what you can do come up with. I promise to refund every money you have spent on me, and even with interest, if that's what you want.

Number 1: Sweetie please I beg you, don't abandon me here.

Number 1: You are the only one I can count on right now. (a bunch of emojis crying and solemn faces)

Then he sent a bunch of emojis a blob crying, mojo BLOB crying, and another hugging bear and a heart.

Number 1: Just want to be with you and be happy forever honey.

Me: I love you so much it hurts sweetheart.

Number 1: Please tell Sue, I really appreciate all she has done, and been doing to make you happy.

Number 1: You are my life.

Number 1: Sweetheart, you just don't know how I feel a day without you without talking to you.

Number 1: I'm dying slowly here, my love.

Me: You are mine too, but I can't seem to have you sweetheart.

Number 1: I need to be out.

Number 1: I really promised to spend Christmas holidays with you, my love me being here means I won't.

Number 1: I told you I am a man of my words.

Me: You are the one who can save me now!!!!! I love you.

Number 1: Sweetheart, please I beg you for, you find a way to Get Me Out of here, and I will be forever grateful to you, my wife. Sent an emoji again that he always did.

Me: Sweetheart, I have nothing and no one else I can turn to.

Then I had over the phone to Sue again, I was done, I had enough at this point. This is what she said this is Sue's friend, she is upset, you're asking for help and she can't help she has gotten you as far as she could she can she can't she has gone to the bathroom so I took her phone the rest is up to you she feels so guilty right now if you really loved her you'd look somewhere else and respect the fact that she can do nothing she loves you so much it's killing her

Number 1: They are requesting my phone now.

Number 1: Please help me, tell her I love her so much and can't wait to be with her.

Number 1: he's the best thing that has ever happened to me, and I already promised to take her around the world.

Number 1: Tell her she is my world.

Sue: I hope you mean that, and I really hope God can help you find a way.

Number 1: Just can't wait to fulfill all my promises to you.

Number 1: I love her.

Koala hugging a bear again and Sue saying good.

Number one this is for her a Bunny rabbit was blowing a kiss with a heart security guard hello ma'am at least you are being able to talk with your man and I hope you feel better a bit now

Sue: This is Sue, her friend she still in the bathroom, there is nothing I can do from here. She is very upset, and I won't let her have the phone right now. (I was sitting next to her on the couch)

Security Guard: It's okay ma'am please take care of her you know her fiancée gets home

Which you know is never going to happen.

Sue: I'll try but only if I even keep her here, she's just like her tattoo.

Security Guard: good evening, ma'am.

Sue: look I told you she had no money. I had to put her give her a sleeping pill in her tea, she is resting she has done all she can.

Security Guard: So sorry about all that ma'am, you just let her know everything will be fine as soon as she gets hold of her fiancée.

Sue: For your sake I hope so.

Security Guard: Definitely ma'am.

Security Guard: ma'am what's wrong?

Me: You keep asking for money, I don't have.

Me: I'm so stressed out right now, living in my car God sakes.

NOTE: I wasn't but it shows they have no compassion.

Security Guard: ma'am, you do say I keep asking for money, and why would you say that? What is being asked for this, for your fiancée to be out and not arrested over again ma'am.

Me: Then let him out.

Me: If money is needed to do paperwork you can apply to do it, or I guess he is stuck just like me.

Security Guard: ma'am, it's not in my position to do that, and if you are going to speak rudely to me or get mad at me, I think it's best I had his phone turned down and let him remain here as my help isn't needed here.

Me: Whatever, I've tried my best to help, but I guess it's not good enough.

This is Sue's friend you're talking to, she's in the bank.

Security Guard: ma'am if we could get hold of $1050 your fiancée could be out and available as soon as possible, as that I've made sure of.

Sue: Well, you are finding someone else that can help Sue is broke.

Security Guard: ma'am I'm so sorry as I've tried getting across for his contact and only $100.

Stop Its December not too much of a conversation.

Me I don't know what to say. I have nothing only $42.95 Canadian and in my bank. I did all I could I have no idea where to get this money. I guess.

Number 1: Will never get to see me from your words I feel so alone now and falling fast. I have nothing and no one to ask for help, it's killing me tell him I'm sorry, and that I love him very much and that he is an ******* for doing what he did. OK, but I love him regardless of if he still alive and he gets the funds, if he can find me to look for me. I can't promise if I will still be alive because my heart is broken. He promised never to hurt me like The Good Doctor did. I love him, tell him to fix us now.

Me: I am not at my friends I'm sorry I can't guarantee what I'm going to do. I'm hurting alone and I need Number one, but I have no way I can think of to save him.

Me: I did my best.

Me: My days are numbered now because of what the con did and now this my family, if they found out what I did I would be a dead woman now.

Me: Life for me now is living in darkness.

Security Guard: ma'am I need you to understand everything will be fine as your man Number one is a nice man.

Me: I know he is a good man; you don't know what I have been through this year, my heart is sinking fast.

NOTE; Even if you say you want to kill yourself, there is no compassion, they don't care.

Me: I want to die to be honest.

Me: I can't take all this pain.

Me: it hurts so much.

Me: if he has money in the bank, why can't he get it?

Me: I am being tortured here.

Me: Come and put a knife through my heart, or I could take the insulin I have here and just go to sleep, what do you think.

Me: Not supposed to take it if old and don't need it, but it would work.

Me: And, I had lost my bank card somewhere, had to get a tap card which I can't use it wouldn't let me get gas for 20 bucks welcome to my world. I have been in darkness now when is the light going to shine for me.

Me: I'm a good woman, I have helped people all my life, and now the one man I want I can't help, you keep asking for something I will not give, I am living in misery.

Me: I can get my happy ending with the man, who saved me and now ironic is now killing me.

Me: Do you carry a gun, if so come shoot me please, this is not living alive, I only existing.

Me: Listen I need to say this to you, this is not real it can't be, someone who loves a person, someone would work with the person, there must be reciprocation with the person. Achieving the same goal, going to extremes to make it come together. I have done all I could, my heart is broken. I can't fix what has transpired. I care about Number 1, and he needs to get up, do whatever he needs to do if he really wants to be with me. Save my soul this is all I can say please let him know I have never felt so alone so lost then I am now I can't take much more of this it's killing me.

Me: I'm drunk I guess, I'm no use to you, so you just ignore me this is me missing him. I sent a couple of pictures of myself.

Me: I can accept it really, a part of me was hoping that Number 1 truly meant every word he said to me, about his love for me. But it seems that I just loved him, frankly, was the man. I now my heart is broken, I have no one to save me, please tell him I'm sorry covid numbers went up, and I have no way to fix his mistake.

Dictating, Security Guard: ma'am I don't work Sunday, and not supposed to respond to your text ma'am.

Security Guard: Your man is still yet to get the documents destroyed.

Me: Go figure the proverbial loop there's nothing I can do, unfortunately there is nothing short of God's help, but what I can't do is to save him. I don't even have anyone to save me, from me now, its all in God's hands.

Security Guard: ma'am if there was any way getting the $1050 that would help your man out of the situation ma'am.

Me: I am starting to think he is broke, and that why all this.

Security Guard: Not at all ma'am.

Me: Then why can't he get the money.

Me: I was told that was needed to get him on the next plane and this.

Me: When does it stop.

Me: I been to hell, I've seen fire and brimstone literally.

Me: and now this.

Security Guard: ma'am he was supposed to get on the plane but the documents needs to be destroyed, else that will reoccur again by getting detained.

Me: God, please help me I am falling apart.

Me: can't he somehow access funds????????

Me: Wire transfer from bank can he make a call???"

Me: Someone there must be aa way.

Me: if he has money, then the issue, should be how to let him access it.

Me: I know he's a good man, but I the one getting hurt here, no one else.

Me: You must have someone that can spot the money, like a bounty hunter, if he good for the money.

Security Guard: ma'am he needs to find a way to get out before he can get hold of his bank account.

Security Guard: ma'am that was only to get him out from been detained, and if you won't see reason with me, it's easy for me to turn off his phone, and keep that till he is out ma'am.

Security Guard: it's all good ma'am, so as your man can get home when that is done.

Me: So, you know, I have a good heart I've helped a lot of people in my life, and it's hard for me to ask them to pay me back because I know they are hurting. Just as much as I am sometimes. I know

What iT feels like and if nothing else he needs that money for something, and it is who I am.

Security Guard: ma'am I understand that, and I'm overwhelmed with your good heart, and honest as your man is indeed lucky ma'am.

Security Guard: good morning, ma'am, and how was your night"? I hope everything is fine, as I want you to know your man will be out and everything will be fine.

Me: Did he get the funds necessary.

Security Guard: ma'am that question should be for you as his bank account can't be accessed now. Till all of this is paid, I know and said a huge amount was found I his account, but all of that is none of the authority's business, as ones he gets the $1050 he should be able to access his bank account ma'am.

Me: Well, time will tell.

Security Guard: it's alright ma'am.

Security Guard: ma'am never heard from you all day, as I hope and pray everything is fine, ma'am.

Me: Still waiting.

Security Guard: it's all right ma'am.

Security Guard: ma'am I'm sorry still haven't had any positive response from you, yet as I want you to know as the day goes by it getting worst.

Me: I can only do what I can do if you push me doesn't matter. I only one person with no income trying to help, I can only do so much.

Security Guard: It's alright ma'am.

Security Guard: ma'am just saying, so as we can get your man out for you both to celebrate the new year together

Me: I don't know how it is even possible

Security Guard: ma'am what have you been able to get so far.

Me: I only have a $100

Security Guard: Alright ma'am you go get a steam card so as I can get your ma'am something with that.

I Never did that.

Me: You know what, I have two eggs, some carrots, and a pear in my fridge. If he wanted to be with me, he would find a way to do it. I keep trying but I cut I can't seem to get what he needs. (I never tried to find a way) I can't go on this way, tell him I love him.

Security Guard: ma'am you can try more and see what you can do.

Me: did you read my message; I am having a hard time here. I hope you working on his daughter, and everyone else with the same due diligence you are working on me. I can't keep this up, I have nothing two eggs carrots and a pear that's it I gave you everything. I could get if I had, I would, I don't so can't, come see for yourselves, if you don't believe me.

Security Guard: ma'am I do believe you, and I acknowledge your effort so far is trying to get your man out, As I must confess you are a good woman, just wish there was a way for me to help before now. I would have done that for you both ma'am.

Me: That is sweet of you but only me has tried anything to help. I can't keep doing it, I have nothing, and people promise to help and don't.

Security Guard: ma'am I've asked, and did some research about your man, and he is able to take care of you ma'am, what he just need now is your support to get him out of here, before he could be able to get hold of his bank account.

Security Guard: ma'am never heard anything from you for days now.

Security Guard: Just writing to let you know Number 1 will go arranged in court in a weeks' time.

Me: God speed.

Me: My phone died.

Me: Sorry.

Security Guard: it's okay ma'am, just so sad your man has a week to be arranged in court.

Me: well, if God wants this to be, if he must be this way, it must be. I have nothing and moving this weekend because my son doesn't want me here anymore, so my life changing too.

Me: I did what I could all I get in nothing, the covid is up over 18,000 a day, so I can't even make money any which way.

Me: So, it sucks

Me: Sorry.

Security Guard: ma'am so sorry about that as I just wish I could help.

Me: I just might do my plan that I originally planned, which I have thought of many months, because that con tried calling me again, you know the one that called me out con me out sorry of $206,000. Its I drive to the West Coast or the East Coast, rent a boat and just say sail away. You know, all that want is that no one will know where I am. I'd leave my phone behind, no stone unturned, instead of having a Canadian man hunt over me. They won't find me; I'd rather just be a speck on the surface that I'm going to leave my style behind this time.

Me: Can you just tell Number 1 that please.

Security Guard: ma'am you just must forget about that, and don't let it gets to you, as he is indeed a scam and I bet the authorities are definitely going to catch him, catch up with him as he has met is waterloo.

Security Guard: Your man just needs you more than ever to get out of here ma'am.

Me: When I have no money, there is nothing I can do, regardless of everything. I've done or tried with COVID numbers being over 18,000 every everything under lockdown. I have no avenues I've used all I could, just to survive.

Security Guard: ma'am just $1050 is what he needs.

Me: it could be $50 if I don't have it I can't do it right now. it's difficult because I am moving as well, and I've already paid what I had to pay.

Security Guard: What did you pay ma'am?

Me: Car insurance, I had to pay rent for the new place, I owed money, so I had to pay that back and I still have another $500 to another guy.

Security Guard: ma'am with all that, I believe your mam should be out of here if you had helped him with that.

NOTE: Are you noticing pattern here. I didn't matter if I had debts, it was what I could send to him. I really think it bad that they don't care about my commitments at all, only what they were trying to browbeat me out of.

Me: Unfortunately, I had to pay those bills. I couldn't let them sit even though you're asking me for money, they had to be paid ASAP and I still owe $500 which I don't have.

Security Guard: And when are you getting paid again?

Me: I only get paid once a month. I am waiting for some money to come that someone owes me, supposed to be pay to me for the last three days, and haven't gotten it, I've tried numerous times to finalize it and I'm still waiting. But my bills take precedence for me, they come first. Unfortunately, I must have no leeway with that. I cannot go into arrears because I can't say that more money will be asked of me. Delays I can't take that chance again it's like the con always something else. I hope he gets through this and wish him Godspeed and love him. OK. But I am only one person, a speck on this universe in a bad way, fate and God and to date, I so far have been the only one I know of that keeps a promise.

Security Guard: ma'am your types are rare, as your man always speaks good of you here, and just can't wait to be with you I believe.

Me: Tell him to repeat these words, I am that I am in God's name because those words are actual words that God said in the Bible. Which means we're all we're all God's children, and we also have doubles so to speak, because we have God within ourselves, if we believe and I'm also moving today so I must stop now.

Security Guard: ma'am when do you think your man can get out?

Me: I have no clue right now; I'm just trying to get myself organized. I had a flood on top of the boxes that I spent cleaning up. I've only had two hours sleep last night, and I'm moving today, and I'm living right now for today. I must do what I must do right now, for me I need the dust to settle.

Security Guard: ma'am you just have faith as you have helped him from being detained, you just try to see to just do this, so he can get out of here and make life a comfortable one for both of you ma'am.

Me: I have a lot of faith in God, and one day I was so frustrated I went for a walk in the woods and as I walked, I felt the presence of God, and the universe, encompassed me and threw out my whole body. I felt the joy and love I was feeling but it was breathtaking, I felt so touched, I know God's here with me all the time, and I believe beyond 100%

Security Guard: I do believe in him as well ma'am.

Me: it's very magical isn't it, it's almost empowering quite honestly, and very humbling at the same time. What he did was the most humane saying anyone could do he sacrificed himself for so many.

Security Guard: ma'am everything will be fine.

Me: I know because I did nothing wrong. I can only speak for myself. I wasn't there, I don't know what's going on there, but I hope to God that it's resolved for him soon.

Security Guard: You just keep trying ma'am.

Me: I do don't give up, but when I you have COVID cases over 18,000 a day and everything is closed, under locked down, it does make it difficult, and when your moneys limited, what are you supposed to do but. I can still smile, and I sent a picture of me smiling.

Security Guard: yes, you are indeed a strong woman, and I appreciate that ma'am.

Me: Thank you.

Security Guard: You are welcome, ma'am.

Security Guard: ma'am it's been days, we've heard from you as we hope everything is fine?

Me: No, I'm not fine I'm hurt, in pain and am weak, my soul is a shambles.

Security Guard: So sorry about that ma'am, just wish there was something I could do to help.

Me: You can't, there is no one that can help me. I'm best just to take and let go and move on. Not sure if you're going to understand me or not. I need time to figure things out, but sometimes that is to be determined. okay it's not that it makes me. it's what I have been through, but I don't think you understand, that is easy to say, let go, but it's affected me profoundly. I need to reboot myself, but sure you don't understand that. I need you to be happy, feel happy, so I am sending you a smile, it may not be a smile that's pure right now. I'm going to church today something I haven't done in a long time, to speak directly to God himself, to help me, and you OK. I sent a picture of myself again with a fake smile.

Security Guard: ma'am I will show that to your man Number 1.

Me: I am always the one getting hurt, because of things anyway, it's just that was my life. I want to be happy, truly happy, only through God, I can trust with my soul, to give me the answers, you know these words, to thine own self be true, well those I will find.

NOTE: BLOCKED

This is quite recent too because the last text I got from them was just yesterday. so, you can see even though a promise is made you, you can still get hurt regardless. Number 1 was my rebound guy, and trust me, you will have a rebound guy, even though you tell him the whole truth of everything that's happened to you. They'll show you the compassion, the caring, the loving, they will make a connection. They will entice you in deep because there's more cons on the Internet than not. They'll use everything in the book, use it differently when it comes to how they retrieve money from you, and they'll make it sound so believable. But in looking at this whole conversation through the last month, what stands out? To me what stands out is that he's a criminal, apparently, he had illegal drugs and that's why he's being detained. Is it is he really being detained, or is it just another ploy to get more money out of you? When someone asks you for money, that should be a red flag to you, right off the bat. Because no matter who it is, they'll take your loneliness and use that to take whatever they can get from you. They want to hear your thoughts, your passions, your desires, the things that make you happy, because that increases your dopamine levels.

It doesn't matter who the person is, doesn't matter what they're trying to do or say. It's how they do it because they put their own personality in how they do it. I do believe that he's using a fictional security guard to say that, oh he's in custody, but remember one thing an airport does not use bitcoin machines. You must look at all the different respectful ideas that they're giving you, because it's a façade, it's not real. If you noticed even with the way I question things, it's not about me, it's always about getting the end game, your money. It doesn't matter if it puts you into debt, or you don't have anything to eat because, they don't care about that it's all. It's about greed and if you've been conned once, you can be conned again. Don't think you can't. I think that's why he didn't want to let me go, when I said you better run, I've been conned, I've got nothing, you become an easy mark. That's all it is, and as much as I'd love to find love true love, I know that this Number 1 is not my true love now. Once you pay that it'll be something else again. It just doesn't end okay, regardless of how hopeful you are, regardless of how much you believe, there's no end. I still have six more I can tell you about its saddens me and it's scary.

PART TWO

Now you got to remember at some point you're going to start thinking to yourself. Therefore, I did what I did, just to let you know. I want to clarify this now; I know it's hard to fathom and people do have the right to worry about me. It's very difficult because the first con opened a door inside of me. It felt so good to have someone show me that much attention. That much love, it will seem like a devotion in a way, because you're put on a pedestal. You are so high at that point, and I know I've used that phrase to him. He loved that phrase when I said, you make me high. You feel like you're on drugs quite honestly because suddenly you feel loved and cared for. The one thing they all say to you, I'll never hurt you, and I'll never ask for money.

Now The Good Doctor for one, he said he wasn't asking for money it was the United Nations asking for money, and Number 1 said it wasn't him asking for money, it was the guard who was detaining him. They're kind of smoke screening the reason as to why they want the money, they're saying that he is being detained; you can't detain someone for that length of time without either putting him in prison, or in front of a judge. Now they did say that he was supposed to see a judge sometime this week, but there was no mention of that. So what, did that not transpire? I'm just playing the game right now because I can see where it's going, and I'll show you. It's been hard; I'll tell you right now and I've had to do a lot of soul searching to myself to get this far. It hurts because men all say things that'll make you feel so good and special, but they don't mean it. They get angry when you say no, that you're not going to do what they say. They try to make you chase them, do whatever they say, because you don't want to lose them. Obviously, you don't want to hide the gratification, the love, the devotion, the attention. That's all part of your dopamine levels. That's something you must look at, deep within yourself, use your gut (its never wrong). Now we'll go on to the next con output column, because that's what he is a con.

OK now let's go to Number 2 now Number 2 is a sweet guy, about half my age, with a son apparently. He's using his son in this little ditty as well because the son's been emailing me, calling me mom, which is a new thing in a way. Not really because I still have others that are doing the same thing, but not to this degree. So, what can I say about Number 2, apparently, he's a Sergeant in the military, he says he's putting his life on the line every day. He's tired of it, that he's been there too long, that he hasn't seen his son for well over a year. He's scared of dying and leaving his son by himself, keeps asking me if I will take care of his son for him. He's asked me numerous times to marry him as well, because he says he has undying love for me. So, let's look at this gentleman now. He did add a twist to his though, he said he was conned out of $150,000 by a woman. So there's a bit of commonality there, he has to find a mutual ground to connect with me. Now in this connection he told me a bit about what he did and what he wants to do. And this one is like The Good Doctor in a way. He said how beautiful, I am how exciting and alluring I was. I haven't known him very long and that's partly the interesting part of this whole thing, let's take a look at our conversation, okay, you can be a judge of it, so here we go.

Now in fairness he did **** me off, near the beginning I deleted the whole conversation. But I'll just take up from where I left off because at first, he was very sweet romantic trying to get my attention. (He used the fear of loss near the beginning, but all he did was make me angry) and got me in his little groove, but I ended up saying to him it's all in the execution of how you do it, because he said he was trying to get leave, and was having no avail with this commander.

Number 2: Babe, I can't talk to him he is very harsh and wicked, he got rank and power.

Me: So, use respect, become his friend.

Number 2: Babe I have been working so hard if the military could offer me a freely vacation.

Me: Kiss his ***.

Number 2: Babe could you believe that 29 soldiers left the camp by military free vacation, my name was among the listed soldiers for vacation, unfortunately for me somehow someone erased my data from the military data device.

Me: How is it possible, I'm sure they can straighten it out for you, did you print it off.

Number 2: Babe, a lot is happening here in camp the military is deadly job, which you might never want me to do, if you really understood what I did what it was.

Me: Oh, I really do understand, I told you I not a normal woman.

Number 2: Babe a lot of people are envious of my awards and accolades here, babe they trying to end my life, but God has been my strength babe, what do you mean, but you are not a normal woman.

Me: I understand the darkness of war, I see the death, feel the pain. It is something God has given me, have had it since I was young. I feel others pain since then, that is why I care about people, that is why I help people, that is why I do what I do.

Number 2: Babe don't worry about that. I got all it takes to bring back joy into your life, don't bother about the money you spent, can give you access to my bank accounts, heart and a rose don't ever regret your life sweetheart.

Me: I don't, I embrace it, learn from it and grow. I have two another gift God gave me.

Number 2: You are blessed to see this day, many are dead, I'm happy to see you alive. I got to celebrate you with my love, with a heart babe, all I want from you is your smile and love.

Me: My friend just told me how unique I really AM, how I can make a negative a positive.

Number 2: Don't text the bad guy anymore.

Me: Smile you are sweet.

Number 2: I love you, so much babe does you love me?

Me: I love you too.

Number 2: Babe I'm blessed to have a beautiful woman like you honey. I need a card for my device upgrade 500, how can you how could you get that fast?

Me: Give me access to your account, and I can do it today smile I have nothing.

Number 2: Babe yeah, that could be easy, it's going to require verification process, due to military policy and agreement with banks, we need to figure it out now babe. I have to update this device to continue talking to you honey.

Me: Well I don't have money, that would like 850 Canadian dollars.

Number 2: You know I love you, so much 500 for updates.

Me: I don't have 200 for myself.

Number 2: That's not the point.

Number 2: I know you don't have money you told me earlier, stop repeating that.

Me: How can I get it?

Number 2: I try to make it home so I could be easier to access my bank account, okay don't feel left alone honey, I never forgot you sweetheart.

Me: How can we get it?

Number 2: Babe I don't really know? You got to figure it out, I got to pay back.

Me: I've been compromised by the guy that guy, everything in my name, people don't trust me because of the ******* so how am I going to figure this out?

Number 2: Babe that's a big **** with a half with a heart.

Me: Yes, it is, I feel more like a criminal than a victim, and my information is tagged.

Number 2: Babe that's not an excuse for $500, LOL text me later the device trying switch off.

Me: it is when one doesn't have it and has one no one who will help her.

Number 2: Get the card as soon as possible honey, with a whole bunch of imagoes.

Me: Bad hair day, but woke up, now lol. (With happy face and smiling myself)

Number 2: Beautiful with a whole bunch of mojos.

Me: It's bad LOL.

Number 2: Honey looks fabulous.

Me: Two funny, but soon the doctor is going to take the smile off my face, ha ha ha I hate doctors, ironic right.

Number 2: Don't mind about doctor's work, your beautiful indeed believe me.

Me: Thanks smile.

Number 2: I love you, I am jealous, (with the heart)

Me: First time I had having two coffees, wow, in add row, I love you too.

Number 2: I love you so much sweetheart.

Me: they never find anything even toys, wow don't like doctors, but I can make them laugh.

Number 2: You are so cheerful. (With a whole bunch of happy faces)

Me: The more I am the nicer I get treated. I play the game, when I broke my wrist, they always knew me by name.

Number 2: oh.

Me: Yeah, even the surgeon wanted to go out for a coffee with me.

Number 2: Oh, you are awesome honey. I said it everyone would love you. (With whole bunch of hearts)

Me: My dentist ended up saying well when you get to be British Columbia can I come and stay with you, I said only if you can find me ha ha ha.

Number 2: That's so sweet. I have been praying so I could make it alive here. I want to see you, have fun together, share some thoughts, and create history. (With a whole bunch of hearts and roses)

Number 2: Hello.

Me: Hi.

Number 2: Babe where are you at?

Me: Sorry getting in car going, needs to warm up and needs to be cleaned off.

Number 2: Alright babe, (unlock with a happy face)

Me: In my room for a couple of minutes, then must go down.

Number 2: Big you got to get the card today OK!

Me: That takes money, you know that right.

Number 2: Babe I know that babe you got to try OK.

Me: that's all I can do right, now is try. I need some time, keep your fingers crossed and say a prayer so I can ask.

Number 2: Alright babe I love you so much.

Me: Love you too, Hun just take it easy OK.

Number 2: I promise you honey. (With a heart that has an arrow through it)

Mel Always, the only thing I can say is let the games begin, that's the best way to put it, well here I go I'm off to the races.

Number 2: Hello my love. (With a heart)

Me: Hello, you are the best and there weren't any toys inside. She started laughing when I was telling her what my thoughts were, (add send a picture of me smiling)

Number 2: Ah baby you are beautiful parts. I'm so sorry for the late reply baby, I'm here now with you baby.

Me: Hey.

Number 2 What's up.

Me: Sorry, had doctor's appointment today, and had running around. I have been trying to get money waiting to see if they show up, no word yet, but she called me.

Number 2: it's okay baby, I miss you so much baby, but I am having a hard time. it's okay baby, when are you going doing right now.

Me: Sitting downstairs waiting, lol hoping they show up soon.

Number 2: My love.

Me: Sorry was leaving or a message.

Number 2: You mean you were waiting for the doctor? No money has shown up baby.

Me: No for the for the girl that owes me money.

NOTE: Another play to see what he say.

Number 2: okay baby,0 did she said she was coming, give you the money she's owing you?

Me: Yes, twice now she's going to voicemail.

Number 2: My love with heart just try your best OK. I believe in you baby; you are always in my heart baby.

Me: She said she would be here at 8:00 AM morning LOL.

Number 2: okay baby, I just pray for her to keep her word baby by 8:00 AM, what time is it over there now honey?

Me: 9:21 PM

Number 2: okay love, please just take good care of yourself okay baby, and have some rest okay baby.

Me: I have been up since 4:00 AM night.

Number 2: it's okay baby, you know you are the only one I have in my life with Number 2s sons name, baby I have just what. I want you to be happy always baby.

Me: Smile.

Number 2: Yes baby, you are all I have in this Lonely Planet.

Me: Sorry, that is sad.

Number 2: It's okay baby thanks for coming into my life.

Me: Smile I am child of God because the shots you know that.

Number 2: There is no words that I can describe my love for you. I love you so much

Me: You are sweet.

Number 2: Just for you babe and you know you are the one that brings that out to me babe.

Me: Smile.

Number 2: Yes baby, I can't stop thinking about you me smile.

Number 2: I love you baby, what are you doing right now baby?

Me: Sitting on my couch doing nothing, going to lie down shortly been up since 4:00 AM

Number 2: it's okay you, are and you really need to rest my love.

Me: Plus, someone set the alarm on my clock, it went off at midnight and when on for an hour, till I figured out how to shut it off LOL, even then 1010 minute had to walk across the room each time that was a pain.

Number 2: lol (Laffey face) thank God you found out how to turn it off.

Me: Never used one when I worked, don't need it now. I know who it did too she went oops this morning.

Number 2: lol it's okay baby, just want you to always be see you happy.

Me: Would you mind if I get some sleep.

Number 2: it's okay baby, you really need it my love. (With a heart)

Me: I do.

Number 2: I'm just here for you baby, text me when you wake up OK. I love you so much baby.

Me: I will night.

Number 2: goodnight my love (with a heart)

Number 2: Hello baby.

Me: Morning.

Number 2: Babe.

Me: Yes.

Number 2: Honey I have to admit this anywhere and everywhere you call me; I would be there. You are never truly alone, because the key to a heart is with you, and I am only a call away, wake up today, and bask in the warmth of the sun, enjoy the refreshment, refreshing that comes with the rain and above all know that my love follows you. And sticks by you no matter the condition of the weather. I adore you, my sweetheart. (with some roses and hearts)

Number 2: babe are you there?

Me: Yes sorry.

Number 2: Where are you at.

Me: Woke up to this. I sent a picture of what the weather was outside because it snowed

Number 2: Snowy

Me: Sitting looking at this.

Number 2: (Snow emoji)

Number 2: You got to stay healthy. (With a couple of hearts) I love you babe, (with a happy face and a kiss)

Me: I got a cold my grandson gave it to me.

Number 2: Babe you got medication?

Me: must check smile, maybe in my room.

Number 2: okay babe I love you so much sweetheart. (couple happy faces and kisses)

Me: it too shall pass, love ya.

Number 2: Sweetheart I love you so.

Me: lol sorry I closed my eyes.

Number 2: Babe (couple happy faces with hearts) honey (with another happy face in her heart)

Me: Sorry I was looking for something, I found it, you need to run from me.

Number 2: LOL (with a happy face laughing)

Me: Run for safety.

Number 2: Honey, I really want you so much, with a kiss babe you are you feeling sleepy?

Me: Yeah, do you mind if I close my eyes for a bit.

Number 2: Babe don't worry, you got to sleep OK. (With kisses and happy hearts)

Me: Thank you.

Number 2: You're welcome.

Me: I just woke up.

Number 2: How are you doing babe?

Me: My son in law sent me this, he didn't see me this morning and he missed me, and it's a picture of him completely frost covered all over. His face and chest and hair, then I said that woke you up by the sound phone call, they never come, right, and I tried calling left message for her to call me.

Number 2: My love (with the heart)

Me: Yes, sorry I may have to clean off my car and drive there.

Number 2 It's okay baby, please just try your best, OK, my love (happy face and a heart)

Me: All I can do.

Number 2: You are my happiness baby.

Me: I had to wake up, lol so I went outside to this, and it's just covered in snow.

Number 2: Hello oh baby you are so beautiful (with a heart) you are so hot babe.

Me: Not now, you're just fishing.

Number 2: Babe where are you at?

Me: Sitting at the table having a tea, smile.

Number 2: Babe, you got to wait for me. LOL (was a happy face emoji)

Me: Maybe the pill I took helped me last night, LOL head not stuffy.

Number 2: I'm used to Mars here babe, I get cancer stuff LOL (with a happy face)

Me: What is that, lol sounds horrid.

Number 2: Babe that's canned food LOL.

Me: Yummy.

Number 2 lol really

Me: lol why they go all out.

Number 2: Babe do you love canned food?

Me: I prefer real cooking but depends on the taste me. I could live on boiled eggs LOL.

Number 2-: oh, babe you loved boiled eggs. (With a happy face)

Me: LOL no, but they are cheap and can keep you alive.

Number 2: Really>

Me: Really, that's been my life for months.

Number 2: You got to make it easy though, make how could you feed on that?

Me: Yeah, when they're just me, it's easier, smile, one egg for morning maybe an egg for lunch and an egg at dinner LOL.

Number 2: Babe if you received your money today you got to buy food stuff OK.

Me: LOL not right, I put out fires for others remember.

Number 2: Babe, why not right?

Me: I keep other people's lives normal.

Number 2: You don't feel well babe, that's nice your life should be nice too.

Me: Not me lol never was sweetheart, one outweighs the means of the many.

Number 2: I don't trust that.

Me: why?

Number 2: You are confusing me.

Me: Only one suffers for many, this way.

Number 2: Babe alright, do you enjoy eating boiled eggs?

Me: That's why God comes to me smile, no, do you enjoy canned food.

Number 2: Babe, I don't really but I have to because I'm in in the camp.

Me: I see no different, smile because the cause outweighs the means.

Number 2: Hello baby, sorry for the late reply.

Me: How are you doing, it's cold outside.

Number 2: Just that this, my device baby. I need to upgrade it baby, it's given me a lot of problem here you need to take good care of yourself baby.

Me: I always take care of myself, no one else will.

Number 2: it's okay I will be there soon to help you baby.

Me: That's so sweet of you to say. I don't have a bed in my room just the couch.

Number 2: Yes, baby believe me OK.

Me: I left my bed behind because it was only a day bed anyway so.

Number 2: Don't worry about that baby I will take care of that OK.

Number 2: Babe where are you at, who are you texting.

Me:? A friend apparently, she at the hospital now, lol that's why she didn't come this morning.

Number 2: Babe.

Me: LOL she always has an excuse.

Number 2: Babe it okay don't feel bad about that OK.

Number 2; I'm trying babe, I love you.

Me: Smile, love you too.

He sends me a bouquet of flowers and a picture.

Me: Ah.

Number 2: I can't stop thinking about You. Beautiful love it makes me feel so humble to you sweetheart. You are the woman of my dreams, very caring to the to my soul and response that the language of the heart. (With a whole bunch of hearts and roses)

Me: never had that much attention.

Number 2: Babe I never had a beautiful woman like you. You make me feel so happy and comfortable with your sweet love. I hope to preserve your sweet fragrance. (With a whole bunch of hearts and then a batch of roses)

Me: Smile.

Number 2: Honey (with happy faces and hearts) do you believe I love you so much.

Me: I really do LOL; you've done things for me and don't know how much. yeah, The Good Doctor hasn't tried contacting me, I am so happy. I don't like mind gamesokay, that's what he was doing, and I was******* with him. He is a narcissist because once I gave you my email info, he stopped thank you.

Number 2: I love you babe. (With some happy faces and kisses)

Me: Smile it was it, wasn't it?

Number 2: Babe I'm glad it was successful.

Me: With him out of the way I can move forward.

Number 2: Babe that is so sweet, babe don't contact him again.

Me: it's true I don't, and with the new number he doesn't have. He can't send messages through my phone.

Number 2: You have taught me to be fearless in love and what it means to love with total abundant. it was a hard bit for me everything and anything is worth you. My future is bleak with you to be my sunlight and illuminate. My steps in the right direction, I love you with all of me my darling. Best wishes for you (little bunch of hearts happy faces and flowers)) I'm strongly in love with you sweetheart. if loving you the way I do is wrong then I don't want to be right. I just want to keep on loving you with as much passion as I possess now.

Me: Can I ask you something.

Number 2: Babe all right.

Me: How did you did do it, sorry my inquisitive side talking. I knew for a while just didn't ask.

Number 2: I work with the military information department. I find it easy to communicate with you through the device it's prohibited here to access cellphones.

Me: Oh. I see I'm impressed which means The Good Doctor was doing many illegal things.

Number 2: Babe he was trying to ruin you, sweetheart but thank God saved your humble soul.

Me: I'm grateful for those thanks be to God. Amen. He wasn't trying he already ruined me, he destroyed me in honesty. My only saving grace is I'm not materialistic or anything like that, but right now I'm just trying to survive.

Number 2: Babe that's good how much do you have all now?

Me: Now its 22,000 it was over 80,000.

Number 2: Babe, how will you pay the 22,000 seems very difficult for you.

Me: I've been doing a monthly payment right now. it's the only way I can do it now.

Number 2: Alright babe don't worry about that.

Me; I have to it's my debt, I've always paid my debt.

Number 2: I know but you got to take it easy.

Me: But I also had excellent credit at one moment point in time until the *******

Number 2: Your house really matters a lot.

Me: my house is something I do take care of. I'm the only one that can do that, henceforth why you are just enough.

Number 2: Babe he got my new information, right?

Me: what new information.

Number 2: Bank information.

Me: I don't understand.

Number 2: You are completely restricted from for banking.

Me: Switched banks if that's what you mean.

Number 2: That's so bad was a heart alright babe.

Me: the only way I could fix things

Number 2: That doesn't matter right now, you got to be patient enough wait for me my return babe.

Me: You must want to try and keep staying stable, because that's what's important and that's the only way I can move forward. it is knowing that I paid my bills and my debts because they come first to me first, I've always been that way and that I can't change

Number 2: Yes, I understand that you got to do that, but don't let it weigh you down your house first.

Me: It's not the only thing that weighs me down I was trying to find extra cash to help pay for my book, for example

Number 2: babe where do you intend to seek the extra cash?

Me: And that I must rely on others who are old to me. I really don't care if I get my money back from some of the people, but when someone asked me for help, I feel lost and discouraged, because helping someone is important it is just something that I do. I don't know how to explain it, how it feels to me, but I've always been able to find ways somehow.

Number 2: Babe I feel like that too, when I can't help you.

Me: And when I've ever loaned people money, I always knew that they wouldn't pay me back. I feel bad because I owe my friend Agnes money and she's not pushing me and she'll never betray me because we were close friends, but have paid her a little bit back because she knows it bothers me more than it does her

Number 2: I really want to help you financially, but it's kind of difficult for me the camp they restricted my access to bank.

Me: Yeah, I really know the drill trust me. I've heard every excuse in the book from you know who and a few others before you.

Number 2: Babe how much do people owe you now.

Me: I just completely lost track, let's just say a lot anyway, this has been going on for years it's not just something I just started OK. You don't want to know for sure, but I've always sacrificed for everyone else.

Number 2: Babe I have host charity programs then you know.

Me: And when I say the word sacrifice, I'm not just saying it casually, I'm saying it literally, because I have given up a lot just for others.

Number 2: I do get it before humanity don't get discouraged.

Me: Oh, I'm not discouraged, and I do it for humanity as well, for the safety of others, for the love of others. I never look for gratitude or gratification by any means. I just leave a little mark to help someone, put a smile on someone's face or children faces. Which I have done for a lot, because I love people and not for any retribution in my life at all. I do it and I don't expect anything.

Number 2: That's so sweet honey, (happy face) I appreciate that a lot.

Me: it's the truth, I'm sorry to say, it's just a part of who I am.

Number 2: Babe, that's what it takes to be godsent, don't give up to your cause, continue to bless with little you can afford to do.

Me: I always seem to do the right thing.

Number 2: Babe I know that I have been praying for you too.

Me: Hang on just putting my clothes in dryer.

Number 2: Alright babe. (Happy face and heart)

Me: cleaning just never seemed to stop, every day, sink full of dishes and you know that right.

Number 2: Babe you work with your satisfaction.

Me: You could say I'm anal about it because that's where you make food and eat.

Number 2: I guess.

Me: it's my Achilles heel.

Number 2: Babe, you want me to make you food for you?

Me: Can you cook, but I will do the cleaning behind you.

Number 2: I got to make some delicious. (Happy face) you going to like, sweetheart (kiss in a heart)

Me: You are sweet, if it's not asparagus I break out in a rash for that. I love it, it just doesn't like me.

Number 2: Babe, are you kidding me? How do you clear your debt? Do you get business?

Me: Wait, I'm not sure what you're talking about, sorry my daughter is talking to me at the same time.

Number 2: Babe text me in a bit.

Me: OK, no problem.

Number 2: You got to give answer to my question babe. (Happy face carts)

Me: I have a pension I'm using to clear my debt; it's called Omar's, it's a retirement savings program.

Number 2: Oh, baby how does that work?

Me: Well, my late put into it for the last 20 some odd years, prior to this death and I was his next of kin, so I was entitled to it. I get a monthly pension from it, plus I also get death benefits from them.

Number 2: You know I don't believe in all that this pension baby, because I make a lot of money, a lot of that LOL.

Me: Well, right now is the only way I can survive. The woman who did my debt or consumer proposal said I was lucky that I have that, because that's my saving grace.

Number 2: My beautiful wife there we go.

Me: So, I have enough to get what I need. Not compared to many of them who have been conned. There are many over the years the that committed suicide, left out on the streets, homeless, distraught, and depressed. I am one of the lucky few that can still survive.

Number 2: How do you get a death benefit from them; lol it sounds funny.

Me: It's something that the Canadian government did, part what we paid into when we start paying taxes here. You normally get it when you're 65. But if you have a spouse, and that passes away so that helps and then I get a pension on top of that, but for the most part I don't really care about the money, I lost. I just care about my debt to clear it so that I can clear my name again.

Number 2; Yeah baby, it's okay my love it's a heart.

Number 2: You know I'm trying to understand what all this means baby.

Me: Do you have any understanding of what it means now, or did I clarify that issue for you.

Number 2: I want to promise you that I will take care of your debt baby, once I'm back to you.

Number 2: Yes, baby you try to lol.

Me: I tried to, or I accomplished, which one is it, between the two death benefits I make just over 30,000 a year does that clarify it.

Number 2: Trying to make it to Canada. I want to know more babe. How could do that?

Me: Hang on, my daughter putting her Wi-Fi on for me.

Number 2: Alright babe, (with a happy face kiss) do you live with your daughter?

Me: It mandatory, where he worked right now, yes.

Number 2: okay babe.

Me: Sorry Joe wants me to watch a show called the book of Boba Fett with them downstairs. So, I can give you a break if you want for me. And I guess I should be a little sociable with them, considering they are letting me stay here for now.

Number 2: Alright babe, you got to do that. I love you so much. (with two happy hearts)

Me: I love you too sweetheart be safe.

Number 2: Hope you won't keep me waiting!

Me: I'll try not to keep you waiting I promise.

Number 2: sent me back to roses with saying my love for you have to believe in my words baby, and then another picture with three roses in it.

Me: I do LOL.

Number 2: okay thanks baby, that is what makes me feel so special baby.

Me: Hey.

Number 2: My sweet friend and love. (With kisses and happy faces and flowers and hearts)

Me: Smile.

Me: Sorry, He wanted me to see the first episode. LOL, his sister said something that shocked me. He told her before she met me that I was a hot Mama. He didn't don't know I know, he said that lol. I guess when you are dating a girl you like you look at the mother LOL. I've known this for years.

Number 2: Babe I don't understand LOL.

Me: Well J my son in law, told his sister Sue the one I talked to, that I was hot many years ago. J is married to my daughter, does that make it clear enough.

Number 2: K babe.

Me: LOL.

Number 2: Babe, I'm sorry got a lot of work stress.

Me: Go ahead, I understand OK, be safe.

Number 2: My wonderful love, (with two hearts) you always understand my pains.

Me: Smile, it who I am love you, night.

Number 2: I love you so much.

Number 2: Sleep evades me at night, it's a wonderful, it's a wonder, I am able function at optimum level. You are the reason why I am sleep deprived, and why I function at my best. I want to be the kind of man deserving of you, and yet, I can't stop thinking about you. (With a heart and two kisses)

Me: You are sweet, but you sleep, smile. I love you.

Number 2: You've made me feel secure and built confidence in me to face life more courageously and achieve my dreams in life. You have turned around my life most adore, adorable, my sweetheart I owe you a lot, and I will cherish you forever and always.

Number 2: Hello babe. (With two happy faces)

Me: Yes sweetheart.

Number 2: Babe I'm done with stressful work for now.

Me: Smile, OK.

Number 2: Babe, POF what's that??

Me: You must be tired, something my daughter and I and her sister-in-law put on my phone I've deleted 1700 so far.

Number 2: Babe do you got the password.

Me: Don't ever open Nope didn't put it on.

Number 2: They are sending you messages, I want to stop and hope you don't mind, LOL

Me: No, go for it mostly perverts or cons, I don't bother.

Number 2: Babe alright you got some information left babe.

Me:?

Number 2: You got to log in a new POF. I want to stop their messages on your device.

Me: okay how do I do that? I don't want more crap. LOL

Number 2: You got to install POF.

Me: Really.

Number 2: Sign in.

Me: Then what.

Number 2: And send the password to me babe. *

Me: it's on my phone, hang on.

Me: I don't go in but found out how to turn off notifications.

Number 2: Babe you got to click on the POF, if you found it in your phone.

Me: **** really.

Number 2: What's your username?

Me: My name, I guess Suzanne or email?

Number 2: Babe, what's the email.

Me: I gave him my email.

Number 2: Alright babe, babe you got to wait.

Me: OK.

Number 2: What's the password?

Me: I don't know.

Number 2: Alright babe.

Me: I just went in to see LOL

Number 2: Did you get any code?

Number 2: A 6-digit code?

Me: 037264 sorry went to the bathroom.

Number 2: Babe you don't have to say sorry, lol (with three hearts)

Number 2: Babe I want to disable the POF, right now.

Number 2: Hope you don't mind?

Me: My phone beeping, LOL go ahead, I don't care LOL.

Number 2: Babe, I got to do it later OK.

Number 2: Babe let me have your number?

Me I gave him my phone number.

Number 2: Babe, I feel a headache LOL.

Me: Why?

Number 2: A lot of stress, babe.

NOTE: He found out I wasn't kidding, that there were a lot of men trying to get my attention.

Me: Because of me.

Number 2: No babe.

Number 2: Work.

Me: Sorry.

Number 2: You can't be stressed to me, my love.

Number 2: Babe you got to delete the POF app now.

Me: Really all I know is POF is a pain in the *****, I told them I got to going to shoot them.

Me: How?

Number 2: You must delete it from your phone? How?

Number 2: Babe, press the hold app to delete it.

Me: okay deleted see, send a screenshot.

Number 2: Babe we did it. (With two hearts)

Me: Cool, all I know was getting a lot of BS from it, what was the password.

Number 2: The only thing I want right now is your presence. I want, and I might not always tell you my feelings, but the look you give me when I kiss you mesmerizes me. Your eyes are so full of love just as the ocean are full of water. I will always cherish love care and respect you.

Number 2: Babe, I guess the second.

Me: lol you are sweet.

Number 2: The little things that you do put a smile on my face, you are the reason I believe in soulmates. You are the reason I have fancy love songs. I am immensely blessed to have. (With a whole bunch of hearts and roses) A girl like you on my side, I can't ask for anything better than you in my life. I will treasure you like a Kingdom comes. (With all bunch of hearts kisses happy faces roses)

Me: Ah.

Number 2: (Hearts, roses, happy faces babe) Baby, always take it easy, never stress yourself over petty issues, never lose yourself by trying to do something you cannot be, slow and steady in whatever you do. That will always make you win the race. Always take your precious time to do everything, best you can take care of my love. I treasure you. (With hearts and happy faces and roses and kisses)

Me: Sounds like you're saying goodbye, (I sent him a picture of a friend of mine)

Number 2: Baby I want you to delete Skype baby, since you are here for each other baby.

Number 2: What do you think?

NOTE: See what he's doing, his trying to get me away from any media. I knew what he was doing. Plus, he will ask for money again. I haven't gotten that card he wanted; I know it's coming.

Me: That's my friend.

Me: okay done are you saying goodbye.

Number 2: No baby, I'm here with you sweetheart. (With kisses)

Me: What's app, I use for my daughter

Number 2: WhatsApp.

Me: What's wrong with Skype, yeah, the one in British Columbia.

NOTE: He seemed to know what to look for, to pull me away from communication. I would say I did just to get him off it.

Number 2: Babe, you got to use WhatsApp.

Number 2: Babe, do you know being far away from you is the most awful and hardest thing I have endured, and at this moment I know we are destined together, and being apart brings me great pain. And I will not be normal until I see your beautiful face for, I feel a piece is missing in my body until I hear your sweet voice of silk once again. I will keep on missing you more than I have ever missed any person in my life.

NOTE: Can you notice this, he is making it sound like we have met face to face. He is trying to get me to believe that its real. But as I told you the Internet is virtual, it's not real.

Me: Wow that is beautiful, thank you, I'm very touched.

Number 2: It doesn't matter the distance between us, but the most important thing ever, and every day is that your love dwells in my heart, and I cannot be broken easily. As long as I am the boss, only your attachment will be secure in my heart.

Me: Smile okay boss.

NOTE: I made a point of saying boss, that word bothered me as soon as I read it.

Number 2: Babe, someone have someone here in the camp said I'm crazy about you. I told him I want to spend the remaining days of my life with you. I always desire to hold you, your hand, when you want, and be your shoulder to lean on, and be my all-time friend. I will take care of you dear, dearly to my last breath. (With a whole bunch of hearts and roses)

Me: You're the best smile I feel, wow when we talk sorry.

Number 2: Honey, do you know that time seems to stand still whenever I see your text. The mere sight of you pulls and puts a stop to my heart, and I knew I'd caught the love fever. When I become speechless, whenever I remember your smile and harmless soul. I can't seem to have enough of you, you are my special someone. (With hearts roses happy faces kisses)

Me: Sweetheart, can't believe the depths of what you are saying it's so empowering melts my heart. I'm not sure why God did this to me, why I deserve someone so special as you. I'm speechless in a way. I'm very humble, but I think you're a wonderful man, and you deserve love true love. Hold on to it forever and feel passionate love. To be able to be happy and free of any regrets, remorse, or darkness, just feeling happy I love you.

Number 2: I wish every man in the world would have a caring loving woman like you, but then on second thought, I would be jealous, so jealous. If the that ever happened, you are mine forever. I do not want anyone else to enjoy the love you give me. (With happy faces hearts roses and kisses)

Number 2: Babe this device is lagging and keeps requesting update, and it could log out soon.

Me: Hello, I'll let you go for now OK, you take care of yourself and have a good night, stay safe.

Number 2: Babe, when are you going to update the device.

Me: Whenever I can get some money.

Number 2: Babe, I wish it could understand that we don't have money now, but it's the device, and it can get my information logged out.

Me: Without money, I can't do anything I'm sorry.

Number 2: Babe, don't be sorry okay me, I'm sorry.

Number 2: it's never your fault, me well if I lose you, I'm sorry.

Number 2: What do you mean babe?

Me: Forgive me OK, well you can't talk to me if you lose me.

NOTE: Fear of loss.

Number 2: Babe I'm not going to lose you. (With a couple of hearts)

Number 2: Nothing will stop me from loving you. (Three hearts)

Me: You won't be able to talk because, of your device.

Number 2: You know I can get as many as the card. I'm blessed financially my God's grace.

Me: Smile unfortunately a con took all mine,

Number 2: I'm being stressed because of the hectic camp life, which I believe God will help me.

Number 2: Babe I won't last, it won't last forever, smiles towards the brighter future. (Two hearts)

Number 2: You are peaceful woman

Number 2: sent a ring with a wedding band picture.

Me: Time has a catalyst, God plans our God's plans, things happen for reason lay as we accept it. Embrace God's path, and life will always endure, and love conquer, that is my belief as I believe in God solely, things happen for a reason, and we have to expect the path God gives us, the one God gives us for only his way is the true way.

Number 2: I love you (two hearts)

Number 2: Babe you got trust wallet?

Me: Yes and no, have not you said nothing in it.

Number 2: I was thought up to set up investment in coin, but I don't know how it works LOL.

Number 2: let me see how it works.

Number 2: You are my heartbeat; I can't live without you. (Two happy faces)

Me: Hey.

Number 2: My beautiful wife.

Number 2: Among all the women of this world, you are God's best design, you are the proof that the word true love Is my love, my joy, my life, my sunshine. I will always treasure you, good morning sweetie.

Me: Good morning my love.

Number 2: How are you?

Me: I'm OK, don't want to complain LOL.

Number 2: My love.

Number 2: You know I miss you so much baby.

Me: I miss you too.

Number 2: Baby, you are so sweet.

Number 2: I'm thinking about you baby.

Me: Smile.

Number 2: My love.

Me: Yes.

Number 2: I just want to be there with you baby.

Me: I've come to the conclusion that wearing a nightie in the middle of the winter, is not a good idea with no panties is a little drafty outside smile.

Number 2: lol

Number 2: I love you so much baby.

Me: Hang on, daughter out.

Number 2: okay baby

Number 2: Can you still text me or later?

Me: okay smile.

Number 2: Love you baby.

Me: sorry a friend of mine had a stroke and asked me if I could go to the hospital, so I must run out, bear with me. Well, she has a blood clot on her lung, and kidneys are failing, and she had a stroke, and she only 50 figures. She wanted to thank me. because I was always there for her just in case she dies. She wanted me to know that she was sorry if she doesn't make it, because she owes me money, and as it is, she wanted me to see her face, and talk to me directly, that my dear it's just life.

Number 2: Hello babe.

Me; Hi.

Number 2: Babe I'm sorry for the late response.

Me: That's OK.

Number 2: Babe (with a happy face with hearts on it)

Me: Yes.

Number 2: Babe, you don't show me how trust wallet works.

Me: That's because, I haven't completed it yet. I need to get money, so that I can finish it and buy what I need to buy, so that I can invest.

Me: Give me a bit I'm still driving OK.

Number 2: Alright babe (with two happy faces)

Me: I wrote a poem and I'm just going to send it to you.

> Fear
> Fear is a catalyst in life you see
> It brings out the worst in you and me
> The unknown, the hate, betrayal, and more
> Envelops our lives and deepens are sore
> How do we change it? What must we do?
> How does one conquer, what's worse than the flu!

So many variables so many things
The emotions inside, the shadows it brings
Acceptance to me may make it all right
I look at fear and just say goodnight
You cannot defeat me. You cannot get in
To fear I will conquer, for its life big sin

Number 2: My love (with a heart) you are always in my heart baby.

Me:

There is a time in life you see
Where caring is deep in inside of me
Humanitarian yes, I am
For people is, who I really AM
Sometimes one person can change a path
Sometimes some people will just do math
But it's up to us to find our youth
And then we just must expose the truth
The darkness that is held inside
We need to stand and not to hide
Days will pass, then months you'll see
You wonder if there is really you and me

Me: My words come out better in rhymes sorry.

Number 2: Babe you sound so inspired.

Me: I find through poetry is the best way I can express myself. My feelings, and how I truly feel inside. One day I will publish my poems. I have over 60 of them, so I know I got more than enough.

Number 2: Babe you are really good at that.

Me: it's the best way to express me.

Number 2: Babe what are you doing?

Me: Was driving sorry.

Number 2: it's okay baby.

Number 2: I miss you so much baby.

Me: Smile, sorry then I just needed a few minutes to myself. I apologize I just needed to refocus.

Number 2: Hello.

Me: Hi.

Number 2: How are you doing babe.

Me: I'm OK.

Number 2: That's good.

Number 2: Babe where are you at?

Me: I'm in my room how are you.

Number 2: Babe you got a beautiful memory.

Me: My puppy got sick after my hubby died, and had his eye removed sent a picture of the dog.

Number 2: Oh, so sorry.

Me: This one had a cyst on his leg, and after they were close to him. I gave them to a couple after they had surgery, because I couldn't bear watching them hurt. He was in firm, and they took to the guy. Smokey would only go up the stairs if I went with him but would fall. I didn't want him hurt, and Toby was his best friend. I had to let them both go together, cost a lot to have them fixed with surgery, poor things.

Number 2: Babe where are the dogs now?

Me: I gave them to a couple because they didn't have stairs, smile and Smokey adored them, it broke my heart.

Number 2: Alright babe.

Number 2: Hello babe, you are you look beautiful. (With three happy faces and hearts)

Me: Yes thanks.

Number 2: Honey did you hear from the lady who was owing your money?

Me: No not yet I text her.

Me: Just chilling, lol I picture of me lying in the sun you know dress.

Number 2: Babe you look beautiful (with hearts and happy faces)

Number 2: Honey, when did you hope to pay the 22,000.

Me? When I have money, right now it's going to take me 5 years LOL.

Number 2: Yes babe, do you understand me?

Me: Well 4.5 now.

Number 2: lol babe.

Number 2: Can't you just let me help you with that??

Number 2: But when I get money, I'm going to be paid quicker LOL.

ME: When money that God gives me and pay things off.

Me: How???

Number 2: Babe we got to do something about it OK.

Me: I'm trying my best, really smile. I can only do what I can do. I don't know how you can help me? But I could use it LOL. I never asked for help. I feel like it's the last cloud I must get rid of the *******.

Number 2: Babe I got to text you in a bit.

Me: okay

Number 2: A whole bunch of parts.

Number 2: Smiles.

Number 2: Babe, how are you want to get me home?

Me: I have no clue LOL

NOTE: This was the first time he mentioned about leaving there. Plus, if you noticed it was how am I supposed to get him home.

Number 2: Babe what do you mean?

Me I don't know, last time I did that I was taken to the cleaners, you know that, and I was trying. I thought to help someone, but I was wrong. If that didn't happen, I wouldn't be in this boat I am now. I don't want to talk about my past anymore. I want to move forward.

Number 2: Babe what protocol.

Me: Had to pay for him to be approved for leave, had to pay for his plane lol. I don't know how to do you get to leave LOL.

Number 2: Babe have I ever been selfish?

Me: That's what he told me.

Me: No.

Number 2: I don't understand what you are talking about?

Me: Can't OK.

Number 2: I asked you a question, you came up with the past experience???

Me: I don't know how to get you home OK; I know I'm sorry.

Number 2: Sweetheart, what does my question have to do with your past experience??

Me: I don't know what you must do to really, leave I don't, I'm clueless.

Number 2: You got to explain this to me. (Happy face heartbroken)

Me: You asked me how to get you home.

Number 2: I'm in emotionally exhausted, (broken heart broken heart)

Number 2: Babe are you trying to say you want me to die over here??? (2 broken hearts)

Me: I don't have the answer, no I don't know what you die, I don't know what you need to leave OK.

Number 2: I can't believe you have such evil against me, despite the love we show each other?

NOTE: See how quickly they turn, he wasn't getting the response he wanted.

Me: I don't know how to get you out, what do you mean.

Number 2: I can't just believe you don't want to be alive.

Me: What he did, what do you think, you still haven't said how can I get you out?

Number 2: Who did what???

Me: The con said if I don't help him his blood would be on me.

Number 2: Babe, I don't know how to get out of here. (Two broken hearts and three sad happy faces)

Me: I wish I had the answer. what do you need, must do??? Tell me.

Number 2: What does that mean, are you saying I'm his kind??

Me: No.

Number 2: Babe. you got to call me the bad guy. (Two crying happy faces and two broken hearts) not your love anymore.

Me: He was mean to me and said I refusing to help him okay why.

Number 2: I feel like staying alone. (broken heart)

Number 2: Don't bother to text me now.

Me: I'm sorry, but what is it, you want from me, how can I get you out.

NOTE: He wants me to beg.

Number 2: I'm emotionally drained. not sure I can fix the damage you caused to my soul. Damn. (Broken heart)

Number 2: I don't want to get myself out I want to die here, stop pretending to love me. (Broken heart)

Number 2: You are killing me, sorry I can't get close to toxic relationships. (Broken heart)

Me: That is hard. I'm telling you the truth. I don't know. you just ask me how to get you out, and then you just want went in for the kill. How am I to help you. you're not saying anything. tell me how I can get you help.

Number 2: Babe it's obvious you don't care about me my love.

Me: What is it you, need from me????

Number 2: Don't help me. (Broken heart and three crying happy faces)

Me: I do. but you are twisting it around.

Number 2: I only want God's help.

Me: How can I help you? I'm sorry you feel this way, really, I do. but I don't know what you're asking me to do you're not saying anything please explain

Number 2: Don't worry about that OK.

Me: I'm sorry you feel that way about me. I'm the nicest person you could ever meet. and I have a heart of gold. OK. but I don't know what you are asking for of me. or what you need from me. to help you so. how can I help. When don't you know what it is you need to do? I only told you what I told you because of the whole thing that happened to me, what he did. But obviously my feelings don't matter and to me they do. okay I care about your safety, only you're not saying what you need for me, that a that is a stalemate

Number 2: I'm sorry babe. you got to be happy OK. (Broken heart)

Me: I can't now.

Number 2: What do you mean, what do you want to do?

Me: I don't know it hurts, and I don't know what to do.

Number 2: it hurts me 2/3 times.

Me: You hurt me.

Number 2: You hate me so much (broken heart)

Me: I don't know the process, no quite the opposite, but it don't matter any anymore, does it. I'm sorry I hurt you, but it wasn't you, it's me, I'm not worth being loved OK.

Number 2: It doesn't matter anymore, you broke me, broken heart.

Number 2: You are worth celebrating, but you judge me, and your past experiences.

Me: With an old ***** won't hurt anyone again OK. I'm worthless a has been, not worth the effort OK.

Number 2: Don't love me, till you trust me and believe me.

Me: I can't trust someone who doesn't want to say what you need from me or want from me. When I'm kept in the dark what the **** do. You want from me to do I trust you, but you don't say what you need from me until you do, I can't help you.

Number 2: Don't love me if you can't trust me. Love is worthless without trust, it's a big **** broken heart.

Me: I don't understand but you, you have made up your mind about me. I lost OK. More than you know I lost OK. You have killed me my heart is broken. I will walk away and let you have whatever you need to get to your son that all I ask of you. Is you need him and he needs his dad, be safe and take care, I don't want to hurt you?

Number 2: I don't want anything from you, if not your love, trust, and understanding. I have been through a lot of pain which I won't like to be again.

Me: I must love you; I trust you and understand you more than you. But you don't trust me and understand my point of view. I love your son too he is a sweetheart; he deserves to be with his dad, he loves you so much and I don't want him hurt either.

Number 2 Alright what's the point, I want to hear from you babe, not mad at you anymore.

Me: My point is I don't know how I can help if I I'm kept in the dark. My point is I love you and your son, and I don't know how to help. I can't even help myself. My point is I want to feel someone's arms around me when I'm crying and shaking telling me everything is OK. If we, are we're together, but I can't?

Number 2: I can't feel serious without your love, believe me. I have been a successful man since I met you. I don't want to give up on our love, will you give up on in my love?

Me: No, but I can't keep on going this way either. I've been in the darkness, God saved me. I sometimes wish he wouldn't, but he did three times.

Number 2: They want you happy and hopeful.

Me: I love nature, I help people because I love everyone, I do everything I can, even when it takes away from me. I don't understand, and I don't ask for anything in return? It doesn't add up. I believe in God more than I believe in myself? What am I doing wrong is helping people wrong?

Number 2: Babe don't stress yourself, questioning God for his gifts it's OK.

Me: What am I doing wrong, I need to know to fix this.

Me: I can't get any lower, than I am OK. I don't have any happy memories OK, my life has been hell, the only man I truly fell a connection with my late, and the others other was my dad.

Number 2: babe what do you want right now?

Number 2: I can't afford to stay here see you cry for the pains I caused you. I'd rather get myself killed (3 broken hearts)

Me: God to heal me, and give me life, maybe I just not supposed to have one. Is that the point, is that the answer, I'm here for others not me?

Number 2: You are questioning my love for you?

Me: No.

Number 2: What's your point babe?

Me: I question my existence, you said it yourself, find a happy thought.

Number 2: What's all this.

Me: That would be my dad, but I lost him, I was the last person to talk to him, I was 11.

Number 2: It sounds so string baby, I think he meant strange.

Me: I tried to fulfill his last wish; my mom wouldn't listen to me, is that why?

Number 2: My beautiful wife.

Number 2: okay baby I trust you, and all your heart, and I'm ready to do anything for you.

Me: Told you I'm not normal. I think I feel with her and that I can't change that. I can't stop and when I hurt bad, but then I have my analytical and logical mind. I love God more, than anything else in the world. I feel at one with nature, and the universe. I truly believe in true love, but I'm doing something wrong. I think it's the last piece of me to find that the peace of myself. I'm not selfish, I don't have a greedy bone in my body. I don't know what it, is I'm missing a piece.

Number 2: Babe, what do you want from me to do?

Me: I have no clue. I don't know, I really don't know. I've always had to do things on my own, even when I had my husband here with me. I still had to do things alone for from cleaning, to shoveling snow, to cutting grass, to fixing things, it was all me. I guess I didn't tell you that he left me a couple of debts that I had to take care of to, which I had paid it all off on my own, he had cards I didn't know about.

Number 2: Baby.

Me: He was well over 300 pounds when he passed away too.

Number 2: Your husband had card and you don't know?

Me: I've always tried to do the right thing, because I believe in the right thing to do. Yes he did and I had to pay them off, which I did prior to the whole, if you follow me.

Number 2: it's okay baby, to me what matters is your happiness baby, my love how much is the card in all?

Me: That's what I'm questioning now, is my own happiness. I don't know how I'm supposed to be happy, or what God wants me to do, to make me happy. I just hope he comes to me tonight in my dreams, because I really need answers. I think God is the only one that can get them to me.

Number 2: You need an answer from God?

Me: The cards have been destroyed, he owned owed over 60,000, which I paid off, and that was what I still used when I still had the house, before I gave it to my daughter. I made a deal with them, and I ended up honoring it, because that's who I am. I had excellent credit, I paid all my bills, I did everything right. I even helped all my kids before I died because I didn't want them to suffer. Without many people, over some people's head, that didn't have a roof at all. The time to help people is when you're still alive. With their bills, clothing for their children, school supplies today. But I did it, it didn't really matter, if I had anything for me. I'm just glad I wasn't ever a materialistic person.

Number 2: Baby you are a precious gift from God.

Me: So you see I been be used my whole life, after my father died everything seemed to be different. I tried to portray his last wish to my mom, that never transpired. I swore passed that day, that I'd make sure that every wish that I was given, I take care of.

Number 2: How did you pay the 60,000?

Me: Every cent that I had; it took me 2 1/2 years after his death to pay it off. I got just over 30 some odd dollars. I had enough to pay the taxes and I paid off the loans with dignity and diligently. Paid all my bills that I had. I kept everything to a minimum, but I did it. I never asked for help, A paid every last cent.

Number 2: You do you are indeed a queen.

Me: But I am diligently paying what I can, and lately I just don't have or seem to have enough to make ends meet. I don't know if it's because of COVID or what but I am trying.

Number 2: My love with a full heart. I want you to know that money is not my problem okay baby, you are my everything's a heart.

Me: Hey there was an appointment, wasn't mine either, but things changed real fast. I know God wanted me to see that, he needed me to know what It felt like to be destitute. I understand that part. I'm just lost as that to what I'm supposed to do next,

Number 2: My love.

Me: Yes.

Number 2: I want you to love me with all your heartbeat.

Me: Can I show you a poem, I don't know if you did or not

Number 2: Yes, baby everything for you baby.

Me:

As I kneel upon the floor, I pray to God my soul to keep
I say his words of love and joy, before I lay my head to sleep
I am that I am to give me Peace of Mind
To build my dreams, and rid us from this awful grind
I know his words are full of hope and faith for all of us to see
In the Lord I know he saves our souls for all of us to be
He has filled our lives with abundance and more
it's time right now to embrace it and open the door

What is the meaning of life we all ask?
is it fulfilling your dreams and your task?
is it what you want that makes it that way?
is it the goal at the end of the day?
is it a joy and the wonders you, see?
is it the time that you wanted to be?
is it what makes all things just feel right?
is it the things that we treasure insight?
The meaning I know I will tell you my friend
is created in God's eye right to the end
Man was made, then a woman that will be
To exist as one in peace and harmony
He gave us the power to love and to grow
Happiness in the end for all to learn and to know

How does one look at the soul of a mom?
Is she a woman or someone that's calm?
Is she a friend, a person who cares?
Is she a woman that only shares?
Is she the heart of what we love most?
is she the woman who entertains like a host?
She cooks and she cleans, and does all the rest
But most of all she loves you the best

Dimensions and time are a reality to me
it's bending one's mind, that's set you free
I take each moment as it comes my way
But it's how my thoughts perceive each day
The actions the motives to change who we are
is what makes me stand to reach for a star
So, I opened my mind and create new dreams
And life will show a lot more than it seems

From a seed you see that I will grow

And become the woman that you know
I will live my life with hopes and dreams
Flowing far and wide upon livestreams
Leaving love and happiness joy and care
For all the world to know if I'm fair
It's not how one may find the way
But how one lives life each passing day

Number 2: Baby

Number 2: You are making me to cry baby.

Me: Sorry, I feel more in my words this way, why I'm sorry.

Number 2: You are so sweet baby.

Me: These poems represent my soul.

It's hard to breathe, my thoughts are a mess
Tightness pain devouring me, I guess
How can I cope with what I can't see?
How can I change what's happening to me?
How can I live in a world of duress?
Letting go of that stuff that causes the stress

What is poetry

What is a poem but a self-reflection of you?
In life of the things that we all pursue
Knowledge relief and joy and much more
Enriching one's life to open a door
Let its words in case you like the birds and the bees
Impacting your life like the flowers and trees
Blossom and grow embrace it your way

For change is inevitable each passing day

Number 2: Baby.

Number 2: I want to learn from you sweetheart, kiss.

Me:

I'm just a speck on this planet you see

How can I change what life has for me?

How can I help all those on this place?

How can I change things with human race?

How can I help what can I say?

But a smile I know will go a long way

Me: Last one I promised sorry.

Number 2: You are everything baby I can't leave.

Me: You want to know me read these.

Number 2: Already doing that baby.

Number 2: You are always in my thoughts everything that I do is for you.

Me: Thanks.

Me: Sorry okay I wrote one more, LOL

What am I saying for?

It's all little things in life you see

We take for granted and think it's free

But one thing I know when I open my eyes

is a sweet sound of birds, as they soar through the skies

The smell of the dew as the morning sets in

The feel of the breeze and the sun on my skin

As nature unfolds so does my mind

But most of all I'm thankful for mankind

Number 2: In your smile there is something unique, so, you are so beautiful then the stars.

Number 2: I love you so much baby.

Me: They want to publish my poems too, you know, but I need to finish my book. it's been on hold for a month.

Me: I just having a hard time getting back to it.

Number 2: Yes honey.

Ne: I've been a wreck since I came back from British Columbia.

Me: I'm trying to stay positive, but people and places are making it hard, even the lake isn't the same.

Number 2: Babe what exactly do you want to do. I want to get you out of this wreck and tragic experience, can you listen to me for a minute babe.

Me: Yes.

Number 2: it's never too late to respond to the call of positivity, don't get this falsehood.

Number 2: You are chosen for this, believe me there has been an obstacle to a positive creativity. Everyone who has been a great person, now like you face tough challenges, but don't give up through the devil might win couple times but he will never prevail.

Me: okay God gave me the attention I needed., I know that. But it's what I must do next is it's hard. I know a part of his plan, but I don't know how far I must go to complete it.

Number 2: Remember God is who you don't let the devil weaken your soul. You're with your worst days.

Me: I know

Number 2: Let me see your :).

I sent him a picture of me smiling

Number 2: I love you, your smile is my sunshine, and your kiss is my sunset. Thank you for being the most wonderful friend and companion.

NOTE: Have you noticed like me, that he is still communicating with me. That his device is still operational.

Me: God has, and I know he has helped me when I needed money. He's always just given me enough for what I need, and I'm grateful for that. More than anyone will ever know. But it's not about me, it's what I've been able to do for others, because I've always given up for me for years. God seems to replace that for me, that I know. I know part of his goal is for me to finish this book, and I've kind of been dragging my *** so to speak, because in the book I'm very heartfelt. I want people to understand pain and the torture you feel, the fear. It doesn't get to that point, and I wasn't afraid of my life, it was for those around me. I know I must finish, it's part of me. I think I'm afraid to finish it because it's only because of what it's done to me, and how it affected me. And I know that's going to change a lot of lives and help a lot of lives, because I give people an understanding of what's happening, how he did what he did, or she did. Part of me is just upset that I was able to let this happen, but I understand why it happened now. Even though I understand it, it's still around and everyone judges me or labels me, and that part is real. I know I'm going to have to focus and do it, that's going to be the hard part. The funny part about all this is my doctor at certain people say it's not my fault, but it's not a world where their words count, it's so what I feel from what those that are close to me to those hurts. The hardest part is I don't think they do understand and do it deliberately. I think they're hurt, that it happened to me, but that's always going to be on their minds, and I can't change that.

Number 2: I promise to be your guardian Angel, the one that makes you smile when you're Moody, the one that cares about you dearly, the one that will love you until the very end I love you.

Me: Thank you, I appreciate that.

Number 2: In a world of chaos, pain, and suffering, I look forward to meeting with you again. It makes my trials and tribulations less hectic, knowing that there's a light at the end of the tunnel, at the dark of the day, I'll see you again.

Me: You are a sweet thanks, and I do love you just for your thoughts. I'd want that.

No idea what I meant.

Number 2: Regardless of how successful my day may be. I know that the end of the day I have an ultimate stress relief that I can rely on during my darkest times. Which are my thoughts about you, and the love that you have planted so deep in my soul.

Me: Your words touch me more than you'll ever know.

Number 2: Babe yes, we are imperfect, but true love will make everything so perfect, there are few things I care beyond life the first is love and the other is you.

Me: I'm getting there, trust me and I think that part of God's plan for me, because he knows how afraid I am. To completely surrender myself for your getting close closer than anyone has ever gotten to me, and I thank you for that. I have more respect for you than you'll ever know, your compassion speaks in its words. Words are the words you write, I understand everything you're saying, and I love you for that. What you do and I know you're a man of your word, sorry Sue just called me, and I think she's just worried about me, because she knows I go through a lot. Higher than use you she's probably the next person that knows the most about me, not everything you know though, she's doesn't know how I really feel inside, because I've always kept that personal and private. But then I've been able to do that for many years, until

I met you. So that it doesn't show that I trust you, I don't know what does. I know you wouldn't be trying me and that one of the reasons I do love you.

Number 2: I love you.

Me: I love you too sweetheart and I hope you believe me.

Number 2: Sweetheart the more I spend time with you, the more I fall in love with you, every day you have a very gentle and tender heart that I promise to take care of all my life.

Me: You know that's The funny thing, you are used to never fight or argue or disrespect anyone. When my husband passed away, I like changed, I found out I had emotions that I just never used. Kind of weird really because for once in my life I think I started thinking about me, and my feelings. Its trust maybe they got walked on a lot. I wouldn't have broken. A lot of people and partly because of all that, it was why I was easily manipulated. I understand it now, but I never lost the respect I had. But true right, I don't even know where I'm going with this point. But I guess I'm just trying to justify it to you, or let you know I'm feeling this way. Mostly, I guess because of fear also, because I'm fighting for myself for a change in me. I think I respect myself enough now, and know that I want to, is someone like here. I think a part of me was because of want happened when my dad passed away, I closed off my feelings and my heart so when you asked me to go to be happy place, I couldn't think of one because the day my dad died closed part of my heart and it's been closed since until now.

Number 2: No, distance can kill our bond, nothing can erase our memories from our brain, our heart will always be tied together. With each other since no human being can live without breathing. I can't live without you. I will love you until the day you after forever. It's hard to find someone who is willing to stay with you in every up and down of your life. I feel so blessed to have you in my life, because I know no matter what happens your love for me never ends.

Me: Morning.

Number 2: I don't know how are you doing?

Number 2: Babe are you there?

Me: On phone.

Number 2: All right.

Me: Been doing running around, changing address.

Number 2: What address, babe.

Me: Where I moved.

Number 2: Where is your new address.

Me: Second last call LOL.

Number 2: Babe are you there? Text me when you get back.

Me: Sort of LOL.

Me: Sorry one of those days LOL. Still can't get through to one place. I got to go to the office tomorrow. it's crazy.

Number 2: Babe, which office are you going to?

Me: Revenue Canada, they keep cutting me off on the phone, last place I need to change everything else is switched.

Number 2: it's okay baby, that all is what keeps me going, it gives me such joy to watch you be you. I would never give my attention to anyone else because I love giving it to you. The day when you were born it was raining it was raining itself, but heaven was crying for losing the most beautiful Angel. (Hearts and a happy face)

Me: Going through the back door lol, smile what a day. I'm finally home wow.

Number 2; okay babe let me see your :).

Me: This was before I went out when. I was trying to wake up before I got dressed.

Number 2: Sends me a rose and says I love you.

Number 2: I miss you babe; did you get the card?

Me: Miss you too if I can rest lol sorry.

Number 2: Babe (2 happy faces with hearts)

Me: Yes.

Number 2: Did you get the card for my device update?

Me: No, no money. yeah, try text me if you are there. I did a Boo Boo with the phone LOL.

Number 2: Babe I'm here just feeling bad.

Me: Sorry I'm trying sorry.

Number 2: Babe I'm here OK.

Me: OK.

Number 2: Babe are you playing with me?

Me:?????

Number 2: Yeah.

Me: I don't understand what you're trying to say, was trying to fix my phone

Number 2: okay babe why doesn't you want to get the card?

Me: Somehow, I turned the ringer off, and my son in law just looked at it and called me. I a knob lol, because I need money to get one. Something I'm shorter on. I can get one but won't be activated because I would have to pay for it.

Number 2: Babe that doesn't cost money.

Me: You want 500 bucks. I don't have that kind of money.

Number 2: My babe, will you get it when it's not needed?

Me: if I had money, you would have it already.

NOTE: I did but wasn't going to just give it to another con.

Number 2. Babe answers my question.

Me: Depends on when I have money.

Number 2: Will you get the card when it's not needed.

Me: I don't get it? I know you need it, if I had money, I would get it?

Number 2: Babe are you mad at me?

Me: I'm frustrated really, I keep saying the same thing. I am telling you the truth, but you don't seem to believe me. I don't lie about money or anything**** it so frustrating.

Number 2: What do you mean by that.

Me: The way you ask me is what I mean.

Number 2: I'm frustrating you? Who said you are lying about money?

Me: You said it, not a lot and in some cases, it isn't, but when someone doesn't have it, how in the heck are they supposed to buy it.

Number 2: Answer my question first.

Me: okay you just keep asking me repeatedly the same question, if I was going to get the card and I kept telling you I needed money to get. The card. And you said it wasn't a lot of money, then you kept saying when you are going to get it. When, I went it's not needed? And you kept repeating it. I kept repeating the same thing, I need money to get a card. that's what's frustrating, and by now now how many times you going to keep saying and asking me. It was like you didn't believe me, that I was just playing with you, and not doing it, but it seems that you are playing me. I didn't want to do it but that's not the case, and that's not who I am.

Number 2: Who is frustrating you?

Me: You are.

Number 2: Who accused you of lying? What are you trying to say now?

Me: I feel you don't believe me, hence, if you don't believe me, you think I'm lying about not having money to buy the card.

Number 2: I believe you are giving the man who conned money.

Me: Oh, now you're going treading on very hot water here. I haven't even been talking to the ******* let alone giving him a cent. I have nothing because of him, he's a narcissist an ******* piece of scum, and if that's what you really think, then this conversation is over.

Number 2: Babe what happened to your money?

Me: ever since you've had my email, I have never even seen a text from him or anything and yet you sit here and accuse me of doing something like that **** you I've been******* broke since that guy okay why do you think my son doesn't want me to living in his basement because I can't give him anything so that they can buy whatever they want

Number 2: Babe (broken heart), but I love you (with a rose)

Me: I can't believe you to even say that to me. You say you trust me and believe me. All that ******** and that's exactly what it is ********, you don't mean, if I was ******* with the guy, then you are near the end, only because he was an *******. I wanted him to feel like he was getting something, and then getting nothing. in return. I know he's a narcissist, I told you what I was doing to him. I know he's a liar, the cops proved it to be. They trying to find him, and how dare you even accuse me of such a thing, you don't know how much that hurt me just now.

Number 2: Babe why don't you believe my love for you?

Me: You don't read.

Me: Would you after I read what you wrote me? Where is the truth? Truth is I have nothing and I'm paying for it now. This is day I've got to pay for it for the rest of my life ******* years, for five years. Because of that ******* and the money I got for you your son's card I worked for it by shoveling ******* driveways with a broken hand.

NOTE: Sent a 25-dollar gift card. Can you see it's a cat and mouse game? He says he loves me, listens, then asks for money. REPEAT, REPEAT, REPEAT.

Number 2: Babe we are not talking about money, it's about our love and trust.

Me: Ultimately, it's about money, because you accuse me of giving the ******* money, and that's why you couldn't get your card. That's what you this is all about, therefore how you can love somebody or trust someone when you're thinking what you're thinking.

Number 2: lol you are funny babe, not about money.

Me: But you keep asking me for a card. I supposed to get a card you need money, they go hand in hand. unfortunately

Number 2: It's all about our communication, I care about that but you don't.

Me: Oh, I care about communication as well, but your card has it. Clearly. How you can't I misunderstand anything that you said? I really don't know what to think about you now. You said you were conned, and I thought maybe you might have understood what I've been through. But would you give the same person money yourself, and conned you, that doesn't even make sense at any level. I'm just getting tired of being labeled because that's what it is seems like. I'm getting from you, from family, from friends, anyone I know, that's what hurts the most.

Number 2: I'm just reminding you about the card, why do you take it so seriously?

Me: Because it's a reminder of what I don't have any more. Something I had abundance can't you see that one point. But I gave to family, I gave to the *******, I gave to a friend, and the only really person suffering is me. I don't think you realize how inadequate one feels when they have no control, especially when they like giving people, helping people out, and I think that's what hurts me the most.

Number 2: it's OK, keep your cool.

Number 2: Hello babe.

Number 2: How are you?

Me: Yes.

Number 2: honey seems you are busy LOL.0

Me: I am, I'm tired.

Number 2: Hope you got some rest.

Me: I did, but still, I'm am dozy.

Number 2: okay babe you got to sleep.

Me: No, my friend woke me up LOL.

Number 2: She text you?

Me: Yes, and shortly she will be calling, she always does has issues.

Number 2: I'm sorry to hear that0.

Me: I calm her.

Number 2: Babe you are awesome.

Me: No just a good listener.

Number 2: Babe what are you going to do now?

Number 2: Ay good news?

Me: No not yet and just having a tea.

NOTE: He was hoping I would have money.

Number 2: That's good news LOL.

Me: LOL.

Number 2: yes.

Me: I was right, there working on the 4th shot of COVID LOL. I haven't got my third not till. Sunday LOL, can you say overkill.

Number 2: lol, babe you got to get shot?

Me: I am getting third Sunday.

Number 2: okay babe when last did you hear from my son?

Me: Yesterday.

Number 2: How is he doing.

Me: He's doing great positive.

Number 2: I'm glad to hear that my love (hearts)

Me: Sorry, how do you really block in here, I mean really block.

Number 2: Hello babe.

Me: Hello, how are you doing? I hope all is well, and I'm sure with you in charge it is.

Number 2: Babe it's not well here where are you at?

Me: I'm sorry to hear that, but I'm sure God will preserve for you, help you with and guide you right now. I am in my room charging my phone. You must believe I've got the courage strength and fortitude to do it, believe in God.

Number 2: Alright babe, I love those motivating words of yours

Me: it's all within for you, know that just keep your eyes wide open. Yeah, I keep doing self-reflection on myself, so I understand what courage is. I may not be going through what you're going through, but it's still a battle regardless. The only way we can survive is by taking the moment and seizing the opportunity.

Number 2: Thanks a lot sweetheart.

Me: Anytime, God gives me the wisdom to understand, gives it to you as well, so be strong and steady.

Number 2: Babe, I keep risking my life daily, but I don't mind. I know you are here for my son, if anything happens to me, please take care of my son. I love you so much (with heart and happy face)

Me: Stay focused OK, because it's being alert, that will take you home to your son alive.

Number 2: Babe, I need you to understand I can't do this alone. It's meant to be for us not only me, hope you understand my point? Baby I do (That just pierced my heart quite honestly) I'm always there for you OK.

Number 2: Babe, you are using your past experiences against me? I have never done you wrong. I will not do you wrong. I swear you with my son's life.

Me: I am trying to resolve the issues OK; you must believe that part because. I do know how to love it's does take courage to moving forward for all of us, that must be the end game.

Number 2: You are my only hope of living this hell camp, but you seem to not believe that?

Me: Sweetheart, you just must believe. I'm sorry I'm writing my book maybe a detriment, maybe slowing me down it is resolving my issues, but I must do it for the greater good, just like you have to do what you have to do for the greater good. I just need you to believe for now, have faith and possibility even trust me (I sent him a picture of me)

Number 2: Beautiful. (Whole bunch of happy faces) I love your smile.

Me: thanks

Number 2: You're welcome.

Me: Just stay on course OK.

Number 2: Babe when are you getting the activation card?

Me: lol, when I have money. I only get paid once a month LOL,

Number 2: When will you have money LOL.

NOTE: Now he refers to it as money.

Me: it's not something I get when I want it LOL.

Number 2: Why?

Me: Because it's a widow's pension.

Number 2: That's nice you are lying to me?

Me: And it not a lot OK, you need to believe me. Oh my God really you are asking me that**** you.

Number 2: That's not the fact you are being very wicked to me why?

Me: Do you really think I'd do to you; don't you know me at all. Use your military services and figure it out for yourself. if you're ending up doing a survey with anyone that knows me and has known me over all these years, they will tell you that I am the most

honest person you could ever meet. The one thing I never*******
dude is lie and I never **** with my money.

Number 2: Stop writing all that? Me that's why people come
to me.

Number 2: Are you saying I come to you because of activation
card?

Me: You were the last person I've helped, and that even took from
me so that you could talk to your son

Number 2: So?

Me: No matter what I say you're going to call me a liar anyway
right, and that just makes my skin crawl.

Number 2: It OK.

Me: hello I guess I lost you now right.

Number 2: Not really babe just missing you sweetheart.

Me: What about faith, what about honesty, what about loyalty,
and you really don't know who I am, if you must question me
constantly.

Number 2: I know you babe.

Me: You see I don't cheat, I don't steal, and I don't lie, if you look
at the Bible those are part of the commandments. I believe in God,
need I say more and the only person I've ever wanted to kill was
myself OK.

Number 2: Same here, you got to understand I feel a lot of pain here.

Me: I am also feeling a lot of pain, but I just put on a facade so that no one sees it. But the one thing is for someone to call me a liar or say I am lying about something, that is the one thing that really gets me going. I can be called anything else like a ***** a ***** an *******. I don't care about that because I know better, but the thing the one thing I cannot stand is being called a liar.

Number 2: Stop saying that babe it hurts a lot. I lost my wife, mom, and family. I never begged anyone for an activation card, yeah, you're asking.

Me: Just letting you know with I'm that's being said, it only makes me push away, because you don't know how much it hurts me. Not being able to help someone in need even if that hurts me.

Number 2 text you later

Me unless you were sitting in my shoes sweetheart you wouldn't know what I go through and everyone body knows here that I don't have anything, so they don't ask me if God presents the money to me, I will prefer to help you over anyone.

Number 2: Hello babe.

Me: Hi.

Number 2: Babe how are you doing?

Me: I'm OK.

Number 2: Glad to hear that sweetheart kiss, kiss.

Me: Smile

Number 2: Babe why haven't you text me?

Me: sorry was out, I went for a long walk, have been trying to get myself into a calm place.

Number 2: (bouquet of flowers)

Me: Smile.

Number 2: Hello babe how is you doing?

Number 2: Good morning baby, I hope you slept like a queen that you are, have a great day, I love you lots.

Me: Hi.

Number 2: How are you doing today?

Me: I'm OK.

Number 2: what are you up to?

Me: Waking up.

Number 2: okay I miss you so much.

Me: I haven't had time been busy.

Number 2: I love you so much baby.

Me: You are sweet.

Me: Not sure if you going to understand me or not but I need time to figure things out for myself, what has been going on, sometimes that it is to be determined OK. it's not that, it's me, it's what I have been through, but I don't think you understand that. It's easy to say let go, but it affected me profusely I need to reboot myself but sure you don't understand that,

Number 2: Baby I really understand what you mean OK, but it seems here that don't understand me too.

Me: I know you have pain and suffering; I get it. It's how we're all here and we're all going through something. I'm sorry you must see and feel the pain that is the horror, I get it OK.

Number 2: My love you really need to tell me what you take, may I ask baby?

Me: Someone dear to my heart OK.

Number 2: My love (two hearts) what are you talking about?

Me: You are a very special person in my life OK. I need time to figure me out in all OK, if you can understand that.

Number 2: Yes baby, you know how much I love you, and value you, you need to take me seriously for things to be alright. (Happy face)

Me: I do that, why I here now, that you must trust me OK.

Number 2: Honey you know I understand you more than anyone else in this life baby.

Me: I know.

Number 2: Yes, baby I trust you baby, I've tried to help you baby.

Me: I really hope that I know you are as I am here.

Number 2: (two sad happy faces) I have been in deep pain and depression.

Me: We are connected so have I.

Number 2: Yes, baby but the only problem here is that I'm not in the state. I wish to be there with you baby.

Me: Have you tried talking to your commander or a priest, chaplain, it's Sunday the day of God talked to the chaplain.

Number 2: Babe I don't really know what to do, I think you got to do that for me. I'm so low that I feel I'm Disgusting. (Three sad happy faces)

Me: I'm not saying things wrong, you know that. I want you to be happy you must believe me, and for you to be happy. I need to find myself 100%, maybe the timing is wrong right now. I don't know, not for us to be together. I'm saying just the timing for me feeling the way I am feeling. I want to clarify that, so you don't take it the wrong way, but I do love you, don't get me wrong I just need to reboot myself.

Number 2: Babe I'm feeling disgusting please.

Me: I need you to feel happy, so I'm sending you a smile, it may not be a smile that's pure right now. I'm going to church today something I haven't done in a long time, to speak directly to God himself, to help me and you OK.

Number 2: Babe I'm glad to hear that you got to pray, that you see money soon to bring me back, I'm praying for you here too.

NOTE: See how he threw that in, see money soon, me too.

Me: Smile, I will.

Number 2: Babe, I love you so much kiss.

Me: Patience, please bear with me.

Number 2: Babe creates I got to go to be there with you.

Heart

Me: I will have faith.

Number 2: I'm not losing faith.

Me: You know these words, to thine own self be true, well those I will find.

Number 2: Hello babe (three hearts)

Me: I'm back

Number 2: Hello babe.

Me: Sorry, I helping my daughter give me 14 OK. Hey you, I help my daughter did what she asked of me, but I had to put my brace on, because I had to move things and I don't like put the braces on really. Didn't want to, but I did only because I must, for the next two months. When I am doing certain things however, I can take it off so how's things going with, you are timing sucks.

Number 2: Babe question.

Me: Yes, how are you?

Number 2: Babe I'm here.

Me: Me too.

Number 2: Alright babe.

Me: I'm doing the right thing you know that, just must keep moving forward, be patient, God will fix everything.

Number 2: All right you did well good woman.

BLOCKED

And again, he goes on again and again repeating the same thing, he tells me how much loves me and that he wants me. Then he asks about a card, then he asks about me writing a letter for him, which I did write, but this one here I wrote that his son needs his help, because his son is desperately seeking to see his dad. I kept me out of it. I feel like it was the best thing to do at the time. He goes on saying that I'm a mean person and yells at me and whatever.

See that's what they do, they use you until they can actually get a piece of you. Unfortunately, I know all too well what they're doing, that it has nothing to do with me. Some of them are in the military and they're just looking for a way out. Has nothing to do with me really, it's still one-sided. It's to get themselves out. Which is an unfortunate thing because it plays with a person's heart. I have a good heart and I don't want to see anyone or get them hurt or killed. They're distraught over me, one way or another. For every action there is an opposite and equal reaction.

Chapter Nineteen

MY FINAL THOUGHTS

I'm trying to understand what's going on and why these people are doing this and that's why I'm doing this book. A part of me wants this because I am doing a self-healing process. it's helping me get over what happened to me, which my daughter pointed out. I concur with that. I really do believe that a part of me needs to do this for my own sanity. That I don't have to deal with it anymore, this way I can literally walk away from it.

But I will tell you one thing I was inspired by a couple of poems because of what's happened to me and that's the only way I can express myself deeply. I'm sure some of you are out there, that have dealt with something like this, and are trying to figure out how are you feel about it. Maybe it might help and here's two poems I did write:

> When I stand by the water's edge, I see a perfect day
> I look upon the ocean in just a different way
> I feel the sand beneath my toes so warm and yet so sweet
> The sun reflects on my skin to penetrate the heat
> And as the gentle waves roll in, they caress my tiny feet
> But in the distance, I see a man who works among the fleet
> My heart and soul will wait for him with passion that you see

For I pray I just may have the man out on that perfect sea

The other one is.

As I stand on the shore of a beach
I gaze upon the sun so far from reach
it casts a glaze that filters the sea
Creating an image for all to see
It's beauty and grace just melt my heart
And the tears of joy began to part
In the water now they lay,
For years to come and there will stay
And from the start as it just begun
An ocean of tears that now are one

1

You see what happens is your emotions, they get played with on a very hard, very strong, very deep level. It's not who we are, it's how we feel. Words are the biggest motivators of all. That's what does this to you and me. That's where it all starts, because to start with it's the hormone that's in our systems. it's something that really impacts you. It can either make you happy or can make you sad, depending on how much you have in your system. The dopamine levels, which are your happy hormone. What it is, it's a neurotransmitter that drives your brain's reward system in different ways.

The upside would be if you get praised for good work, where it just makes you feel good inside. And it also strives to look for pleasure-seeking behaviors. You know, things that give gratification, love, devotion, attention, praise, anything that makes you feel happy. And that's what these people do. For starters they try to make you feel beautiful, feel love, and especially if you didn't realize that you were missing love in your life, or never had love. They do try to make you believe that it's true love that you're feeling. So, this hormone is something that really makes a difference in your system. It's not something you realize, but it controls us and gives us that happy feeling.

Words for starters, kind words, beautiful words, in a manipulating manner changes your behavior for starters, because all of a sudden, you're feeling so happy. It's a feeling we all love to have, that you want to keep going. I'm not trying to entice you to get into a relationship with someone that I know is going to be one-sided, but they just know how to do it right, and it's not your fault.

2

Another way to enhance your happy place is by getting you upset. Occasionally as if you notice through my conversations, was that they would argue with you. That's one of the things they do, almost like a push and pull thing. That does happen and it reoccurs, they literally get pleasure just to get angry with you, when you say no to being able to give them money. They put it against you, that you don't love them, that you must prove yourself and your love, by getting them the money. If you're persistent and keep saying no, then they start to warm up to you, make you get closer to them. That's when they start again. They want you in your happy place to get what they want from you.

And then when you agree to it suddenly, they're back to their great beautiful selves of showing you the attention, showing you that they love you. That's what's building up the dopamine levels in your system.

Something else you must look for and be prepared for, is that they'll get nasty, they'll get mean and trust me it will happen. You'll see that pattern eventually, and when you keep saying no, they just keep going at you, because they know that they can melt you down, they want your money and will do anything to bleed you dry. If you let them, eventually they will do it. I guarantee it because they want to get you in that dopamine happy place.

3

Another thing they do is they end up telling you certain foods to eat. Which I have told you about and can look up other foods that do this, you'll know the different foods that you can eat that will increase your dopamine levels. Such as bananas for example, and eggs, are just two of these things that you can eat which helps increase your happy mode. What that does again is change your level of dopamine in your system. It enhances your happy mode, because it's a pleasure food, like chocolate things that make you feel good, which increase your dopamine levels. Make sure you do take that into consideration as well.

4

Mesmerizing words and phrases such as respect, such as because, simple words by themselves, quite innocent but how they use it, and they're constantly telling you how much they love you. They don't even know you really, and they love you. They'll keep repeating I love you, I love you, I love you, and they want you to say it back. The more they say it, the more you believe it, and the more you want to hear them.

They'll use words like connected, unconditional love, I'm with you, we're here together, I can't wait to see you again. How can someone see you when they haven't even met you yet? They haven't seen the whites of your eyes. You must take all this into consideration, because words are the biggest manipulating tools that they can use against you. You must consider all that and take that into account.

Another word that they love to use is trust; they want you to trust them because they say you can't have love without trust. And they keep telling you how much they trust you; they'll do anything just to get you to trust them.

Then it's, we're doing this together, we're a team, we're connected, they try to make you feel like you're a team. That you really are with that person because they really want you to believe, and when you're in love, you do anything; you will climb mountains, you will move mountains, and you'll do anything to hold on to that for as long as you can. This is something that really affects your family, and this is what changes who you are. When you reach the point that you feel like you're in love with the person that changes you, and that's where you start changing big time. Unknown to your family at first, but eventually it becomes seen. It is done by progression, but I'm hoping to stop you before you get to that level. Not just for your sake, but for your families, because it does destroy families. I know it does because that's what happened to me.

5

Just to tell you a little bit of what happened to me at first. I disassociated myself, spent less and less time with the family, because The Good Doctor was on the phone with me constantly. When I was awake, when I was asleep, he would text me. That's the next step, is your sleep process, because they will text you at odd hours of the night. They want you slightly off balance, because when you get off balance you're not thinking straight. Me, I was on sleeping pills, and he talked me out of getting the sleeping pills, he said that I didn't need them, said he was with me to help me, and I believed him, okay. I didn't need them, it wasn't healthy for me, that it was a good thing to get off them and I believed him. Some nights I'd only get 26 minutes of sleep, so yeah it does affect you in more ways than one. Then they can set you in the end to do things that you don't realize you're doing. Things you normally wouldn't do or say, for that matter. This all changes your dopamine levels as well. Your cognitive abilities change, your attitude changes. At first, I did it because I thought I was in love with him, and he was in love with me.

I got scared of him because when I said no, he started to threaten my family, that if I didn't pay or give him money that their lives might be in danger. I even said at one point to him, calm yourself, stab me in the heart, face to face, look in my eyes just once so I could see your face. It's a difficult thing to go through and right now it's even hard just talking about it. I want you to know what's coming, from my heart because now it scares me. I don't want to see anyone suffer and I've lost some family because of it. Right now, as it stands, my son kicked me out of his own basement, and I'm temporarily at my daughter's, but I don't know for how long. I was already at my other daughter's before I came back to war terror. But yeah, you must look at all the angles, because it's going to hurt you eventually. I want to stress this; it's going to hurt you. Please, please, please I'm begging you, take my words seriously, let your family know.

6

Something that they do, and that you're going to have to be very aware of, is there going to want you to stop going on Facebook, any type of media, TV, anything that's going to give you a negative response. They're going to want you not to tell anyone about them. That should be a big trigger point right there. They want you to think that they will be a surprise when they show up. When you're married to them or whatever the case may be that they're trying to do with you. They do not want anyone, and I mean anyone, knowing that they're stealing from you, because people that's exactly what they're doing: they're stealing from you. They're taking away from your livelihood, from your life, and they don't care how they do it, or how much they take. It means nothing to them because they're narcissists.

7

Now this is a big one as well, because they want you to love yourself. They will say you can't love unless you love yourself. You must believe in yourself, that you're capable of loving more than anything else in the world. They want you to believe that you're the most beautiful thing in the world, you're so attractive, sexy, smart, and intelligent. You're brave for doing everything that you're doing. You start dressing different. Start feeling different, you start believing in yourself, more than anything else.

That's a good thing, I mean all these changes, for the most part. They are good things, however how they do it to you is only to make them feel more important to you. I think it's a really good thing to start loving yourself, when I found out that I started loving myself I didn't even realize I didn't and hadn't for a long time, you don't think of you as a mother, most likely, if you were a woman. You're thinking about your family, your husband, your career, money, cleaning, shopping; every single wife does or a mom does. They don't have time to love themselves, and I'll tell you that's a beautiful experience when you start loving yourself. I still love myself now, I just don't love what happened to me. I don't know if you understand this or not, but it does change the person that you are, and loving yourself could be one of the best things you could ever do for yourself. That will change your dopamine levels. And people look at you different, you feel different, you are different.

The people that see you and family, those are the ones that are going to get hurt. We're keeping a secret from them. Don't let the secret get you, don't let it envelop you because eventually the secret is not how you're feeling about yourself, but the secret of why you're doing it and what has to come out, all because of the individual.

I don't want to disregard men in this either, because it's happened to many men as well when a woman starts to show them any attention whatsoever. They feel prouder about themselves, more debonair sexier, handsome. That also works both ways. We can't exclude it and loving yourself could be one of the best blessings you could give yourself, but make sure you're doing it for the right reason, not the wrong one.

8

And obviously the biggest thing is when they start asking for money, or for cards, for whatever reason, they want the money. That you must consider all the facts I gave you, because it doesn't matter what you do, but as soon as you say no, that's when they get angry with you, that's when they try to walk away from you, and you're going no, but I love this feeling of being loved and someone showing me interest. As soon as you start giving them money, they start showing you more and more affection, even to the point where you're doing sexting. And you can't deny if you haven't done it with a con. Because it will happen. One of the interesting things is, when they're having sex with you, they'll get you to promise, big word for them promises, you going to get me the money? When are you going to get the money? During the sexting, they do this, and they want an answer, because when you're having sex we're coming, your dopamine levels are high. Let's face it, it happens, I've done it, I'll admit it. I'm not proud of it but I have. They expect that from you, that's when they know they have you. When you start saying no, is when you get called every name in the book.

9

Now this is a big one, and it's quite simple. Listen to your gut because even if your brain or your heart aren't functioning properly, because they won't be, trust me. When a con gets in your head, they do everything to distract you. They don't care how you get the money; all they want is the money. Now, your gut will be your final answer. I don't have to say much about it just listen to your gut.

In my feelings about all this and why I'm doing this to such an extreme attempt to help. I will let you know. because I've done a lot of reading, a lot of research, and it turns my stomach and in the end, My gut felt it, your body has a defense mechanism, just listen to it.

You see there's many people that have committed suicide because they lost everything. People have hidden from the world, they're just existing, hiding, because it's changed who they were. They basically lose themselves. They feel very alone and that's because they've lost families over it; I understand that completely. There was no support because the families feel like victims, and in their minds, they are, they have lost a part of the person they knew. Basically, their lives are gone because of the cons. Therefore, I'm writing this book. I know it's been taxing on me, it's very devastating and it hurts. I don't know how many times I've cried throughout the book. I can't even read what I wrote right now because it hurts that bad. But in honesty I'm writing the book because I want to help, even if it's just one person. If I can save one person it's worth it. I want to do it because I don't want to see the same effects and results that I've had go through. I want to save you from those effects so that no one else has to deal will all the ramifications like I did.

I need to get it done because these cons are the cruelest, they don't care. They don't care how you get the money, even if you must be a prostitute for Pete's sake. Mine even recommended me doing that, so that tells you how much he really cared about me (HIS SO CALLED WIFE), and how much did he really love me, considering I only had one man in my whole life. There is no love on their part, no respect. In all honesty it's just to prove how many ******** are out there, how many people are taken advantage of— good people, kind people, caring people, loving people—just for their own monetary gain.

Yes, life is cruel, but a narcissist is one of the smartest people out there. But they are one of the weakest people too. They know how to get around all this stuff, they know how to take advantage of you. They will do anything, and I mean anything—well, they won't do it, you end up doing it—to make you become their puppet. Whether it's right, wrong, or indifferent they're going to make themselves the puppeteer. That's what they want; they just want you to do all the work for them and then take your money. But they won't take your money via transfer, nope, it must be other ways by cards, by bitcoin machine, so that it can leave the country in a way that can't be traced. These are things that you must be aware of because it's cruel.

One of the things is I've always done in my life was give people the benefit of the doubt. It saddens me to see I can't turn a bad person good; I always believed there was good in everyone. Sadly, I have to say I am wrong, and I can admit it.

I'd like to dedicate this book to my three children and my grandchildren, even though I have been labeled now. I don't get the same respect I used to with them. I want to dedicate it to Angela Ryan, Pamela Thayer, and James Thayer. My love for these three is unconditional. Their families mean the world to me. I want to say I'm sorry I caused pain, grief, and sadness to any of them. I'm hurting deeply and the emotional bonds and all that was done to me was devastating. But my biggest regret is I feel like I've let them down, because I let myself be taken in, played by a man (could have been a woman) I'm not sure for 100%, but I was taken completely advantage of. All because I felt I was in love with this person so deeply that I would have done anything, I mean anything just to have him.

So not only am I dedicating the book to my three children, I hope they can accept my apology one day, that they could forgive me for everything that's happened. And know that I am truly sorry that I put them through even a portion of what had happened. They don't know how it hurts inside to be me. Everything I've always done, I did for my family and for once I wanted to do something for me. Once again, I would love to say I'm truly sorry. Hopefully in time they will forgive me, maybe look at me as a mom again, without any judgment and maybe have a little respect for me again.

What good thing did come out of it?

I do know now I want to have someone in my life, for me. I do want to have someone to love, and to be loved for me and for who I am. I do feel I deserve some happiness in the end. Whether isolated or not, I don't know, but I know that I deserve to have someone be there for me. It may not be a happy ever after story, but I now desire that more than anything in my life. Even though I had loneliness after my husband passed away, I have never been lonelier than I am now. This does create many different things and new emotions. It's scary I will admit it, I don't know how it'll end.

And just like me, I don't want you to give up on yourself and most of all never give up on your family. I never will give up on mine, I felt reborn and new, but we don't see what was already trying to be happy. I love my children, their partners, and my grandchildren, with all my heart. That part never changed, that was always there for me, I just want them to know but they'll always be in my heart forever.

With all my heart and soul, I hope this does help regardless. I do love you, all of humanity. This book will help you figure out how this happened, why it happened. These pages will give you some insight, or some ammo to help you in this world that you're worried about, so do please try.

Believe in yourself, loving your family, and we'll live in love, but only when you can see the whites of the eyes.

All my love

Suzana Thayer

I would also like to dedicate a portion of my book to those who have been through this, not just for the sake of themselves, but for their families as well. I know how detrimental and very painful, to lose everything you have, to me it's painful and it hurts in this way maybe, even for them. I can just recoup a little bit to get some people back on the ground, that have lost more than anyone can possibly imagine. It's for your soul and you deserve better. You thought you were doing things for the right reason, so did I. I don't want to see anyone labeled or judged because that is for God. God bless.

I found the last part of the book was the hardest, because I really wanted to show my emotions in the book. Not just for the person who was conned, but for their families. So that maybe they would have a better understanding and at least have some closure to the end of all this. With all my love and heart please, forgive them. Have faith and love them because in essence it wasn't their fault. In God's name.

FLASHBACK

I wanted to make a note because I am having a hard time, so then just for people to realize that this can impact them any time; doesn't matter if it just happened yesterday, a week ago, a year ago. There are times where you do have flashbacks because of it, and times when you feel inadequate, times you try to understand the reasoning behind what you've done, even with knowledge, because you can't believe that you did it, and the ramifications that come with it. I just want to read to you something I wrote to a friend in the middle of the night, someone who cares about me and treated me right. This was our conversation.

And it is possible it is possible there is one man out there on the Internet that has always treated me with kindness, compassion, and caring, and has not asked anything of me. He's even said he's sent me something and sent me a receipt, it's supposed to be here tomorrow. I have never seen a man take such interest or care or diligence in my life for me before. And this was our conversation I just needed to say that first okay:

Hi sweetheart I love you so much, I woke up at 2:42 a.m., was lying here, I finally just got up and wanted to say I love you and miss you

I love you too babe

Never for my Princess

You are still awake my babe

I will never forget that, having a hard time sleeping

I am here is there anything you want to tell me my baby girl

Just feeling overwhelmed my love

My book is bothering me

How honey

It seems like I am too hard on myself really, I just want to finish it, move on to the new chapter, which is about you and me, so I can put this to rest sweetheart.

I am trying too hard to complete it and it's getting to me, obtaining the data is taxing on me sweetheart. It's hard but I know God wants me to do this. I just don't seem to have the strength now, is all, but the importance of its contents is greater than anything else I could imagine and it scares me. Not because of the con that hurt me, but the validity and depth of the con. I must finish it for the sake of humanity.

It's seconds me really.

And how people think that the Internet is just a casual and friendly place to chat, but the depth of the cons are very disheartening and cruel.

Babe takes it easy OK.

You are too sweet babe my baby.

Many people have committed suicide over it, many have lost their sanity, their faith, and themselves. Of it I have been very persistent and diligent, logical, and precise, to ensure that the people will have everything they need to have the strength to stop and think of what is happening, so they don't get in that depth.

Am I making any sense?

Yeah babe.

So nice.

It scares me really.

And saddens me.

I think that why I'm different than most people if you get the drift.

Honey just be strong.

Babe you are beautiful and cute.

I know sweetheart, I am holding on to God. I need to complete this so that I can show people and family the ramifications and the depth of all this. I think even if it hadn't happened to me just having the knowledge is mortifying.

LOL

You are sweet.

I love you so much sweetheart.

I love you believe me; we will surely heal the world.

I didn't wake you up.

I hope I can make a difference; I really do.

You will my babe.

Not for self-gratification, I don't even care if my name on the book really. But it just harder than I thought it would be, the words flow but the impact of the words, that is what's hard.

I truly can't even read what I wrote because it's that difficult. I will let the proofreaders and editors do that lol I can't do it.

I have tried to do some of it, but I had to stop.

Sadly, the one that conned me was darn good, but you don't even have to be good at it because it that easy and that is why and what truly scares me.

How's your headache

I love you babe.

You are so sweet my babe.

I love you

I'm trying to be an outsider on this, now just to finish it.

But I don't think I can do that, lol da da da da da da.

God wants me to see the full picture and he will guide me to the end I just have to believe.

Babe, you need to sleep OK.

I woke you didn't.

Sorry.

What is the time there now?

3:51 a.m.

Sorry go back to bed, I will try and close my eyes promise I love you.

You need to sleep babe.

Smile I love you night.

Emoji Kiss

Emoji I love you

A gift of a woman curling up with the guy in bed giving him a hug and a kiss that says. I love you so much with hearts.

And he says love has truly been good to me, not even one second or minute of pain have I had since you came into my life.

Made in the USA
Las Vegas, NV
02 October 2022

56409972R00167